SINGLENESS

of

PURPOSE

Tula Jeffries

BROADMAN PRESS
Nashville, Tennessee

To Allen
whose interest and encouragement
made the writing of this
a delight

© Copyright 1986 • Broadman Press
All rights reserved
4250-29

ISBN: 0-8054-5029-7
Dewey Decimal Classification: 248.4
Subject Heading: CHRISTIAN LIFE
Library of Congress Catalog Card Number: 85-19525

Printed in the United States of America

Unless otherwise indicated, Scripture quotations are from the *New King James Version.* Copyright © 1979, 1980, 1982, Thomas Nelson, Inc. Publishers.

Scripture quotations marked (KJV) are from the King James Version of the Bible.

Author's photograph on back cover by Ken Clark.

Library of Congress Cataloging-in-Publication Data

Jeffries, Tula, 1921-
  Singleness of purpose.

  1. Christian life—1960-   . I. Title.
BV4501.2.J4 1986   248.4   85-19525
ISBN 0-8054-5029-7 (pbk.)

Preface

While we are alive, we never consider that we have completed our course as a Christian. Paul knew that he was approaching the end of his life on earth when he wrote the words, "I have fought a good fight, I have finished my course, I have kept the faith" (2 Tim. 4:7, KJV). There may not be for us an end to designated assignments, or a graduation day in this life, but there are still goals to reach for and plateaus of performance. The Latin term, cum laude, is used on diplomas to convey excellence. If the recipient's work is marked magna cum laude, one receives the higher praise that the title implies. But when one graduates summa cum laude, the maximum effort has doubtless been applied throughout the course.

We all admire excellence. Since all things are evaluated relatively, we tend to judge one person by another's performance. Is this fair? Only if we know the capabilities of both to be equal. In the physical world, the stamp of excellence is most often attached to people according to their station in life, especially with regard to how they make their living. But why should a mechanic or a waitress be considered less elevated for wearing rougher clothing or using more muscle than an office executive or an actress? Anyone employed in honest labor knows when that occupation is honorable, for it becomes, for that person at least, what he or she brings to it.

I often hear the complaint that no one really cares about excellence anymore. An employer says, "People do not feel the same about their jobs as they did when I was growing up. I was taught to give my best; now, they are only interested in 'quitting time and payday.' " The entire nation has become alarmed that our high school systems are graduating many each year who would have had trouble doing eighth-grade work thirty years ago. And if we have any doubts about the disintegration of personal morality, we have only to turn on our television sets any day or night. Like the old question of which comes first, the chicken or the egg, we wonder if the loose moral attitudes reflected on every network are a flagrant attempt of those who produce our entertainment to corrupt the mind or if our failure to uphold higher standards hastened the offense. We can argue that what we get is by devious design or that the producers are just meeting public demand; the fact remains that our entire system, as we think of it, is out of kilter.

Obviously, all of our legitimate concerns cannot be dealt with collectively, but at the root of them is a common cause. This is where our concentration must begin.

Far too many people who embrace Christianity seem unsure of why they are there. All the problem areas of society are filled with ordinary, decent individuals who have embraced God, the church, and "the abundant life." The stragglers of unbelief are there, but they should present no formidable obstacle because "you are of God, little children, and have overcome them, because He who is in you is greater than he who is in the world" (1 John 4:4). This being true, the question is, who is in us?

Contents

1
Move Out of Babylon

My people have been lost sheep.
Their shepherds have led them astray;
They have turned them away on the mountains.
They have gone from mountain to hill;
They have forgotten their resting place

(Jer. 50:6).

Flee from the midst of Babylon,
And every one save his life!
Do not be cut off in her iniquity,
For this *is* the time of the Lord's vengeance;
He shall recompense her (Jer. 51:6).

Everybody needs a Savior. Not everyone knows this or believes it, but Christ is the answer. "Nor is there salvation in any other, for there is no other name under heaven given among men by which we must be saved" (Acts 4:12). To feel the inexpressable joy and comfort of being saved is for that first fulfilling moment all the heart can desire. Nothing in life can ever equal that experience, for nothing else that happens will affect us so deeply. If we fail at that time to recognize all that is happening, it in no way diminishes the changes being worked out within us. That is because we have no control over these changes; we have, for the moment at least, offered up ourselves. Jesus said,

"Except a man be born again, he cannot see the kingdom of God" (John 3:3, KJV). Physical birth is a natural process that occurs when all the conditions are met and brought to fruition. Spiritual birth is no different. Both are operating under God's creative law. Our efforts in either are of no value. "For in Christ Jesus neither circumcision nor uncircumcision avails anything, but a new creation" (Gal. 6:15). In the spiritual birth, we have no cause to glory in anything other than the cross of Christ. We bring nothing to Him but ourselves; nothing else is required but nothing less is acceptable.

When God set His laws in motion at the time of creation, certain truths were established that will remain unchanged, for "God changes not." Man's freedom of choice has always been the dominant factor in his predestination. In the political arena, scandalous disclosures have become common. The media makes much of what this public figure or that one knew and when he knew it. In our finite way of dealing with things, we often forget that God is not hampered by our limitations. He not only knows all about today or tomorrow but has always known. God's knowledge of those who will respond to Him reaches back before the foundation of the world. Again and again we are reminded in the Scriptures of this. "For whom He foreknew, He also predestined to be conformed to the image of His Son, that He might be the firstborn among many brethren" (Rom. 8:29). "He knows them that trust in Him." "My sheep hear My voice, and I know them, and they follow Me" (John 10:27). In the words of Jesus to His Father, "You loved Me before the foundation of the world" (John 17:24).

God is not surprised if we choose to love Him and live for Him. He has always known who would answer His call. Paul had an interesting way of stating it: "when it pleased God, who separated me from my mother's womb, and called me by His grace, to reveal His Son in me" (Gal. 1:16). God has always known all! When it pleases Him, He moves. His ways of dealing with His creation will not change. His laws will remain in operation a million years from now just the same as they did when He set them in motion. He said, "I am the Lord, I change not" (Mal. 3:6, KJV).

Our first encounter with God is at His initiative, not ours. He inserts himself into each individual consciousness in His own unique way, understanding the level of sensitivity in each personality.

Sometimes, He seeks us out for years before we are ready to respond. What a wonderful God He is to patiently keep on calling, "not willing that any should perish." Had He called Samuel only once, think of the blessings that would have been missed in that period of Israel's history when Samuel stood as God's prophet! In my own experience, I hate to admit how many years it took for me to say the words that Samuel, after only three calls, spoke, "Speak, for Your servant hears" (1 Sam. 3:10). Francis Thompson's "Hound of Heaven" was written before the turn of this century, but it communicates a clear picture of modern man's fearful attempts to escape God by his headlong plunge into every known subterfuge. I also fled God through days and nights. The haunting, perceptive poem expresses no new discovery of that period. A psalm of David had already voiced man's inclination to flee God:

> Where can I go from Your Spirit?
> Or where can I flee from Your presence? (139:7).

There must be a common clue in the reasoning behind our avoidance of the spiritual life. It must be fear, but fear of what? Is it fear of the unknown? To find our answer, we must look back to the physical birth. After he is born into the world, a tiny baby finds comfort in his mother's arms. A loud noise can cause the baby to awaken screaming. If he is alone in his crib, he may be frightened. But the moment the mother picks him up and speaks softly to him, he is soothed and comforted. Before he is old enough to have a coherent, intelligent thought about her love for him, he instinctively trusts that love. This is the beginning of a relationship with opportunities and possibilities that can last throughout their lives. The unknown fear in the child becomes invalid in the mother's arms because it is not unknown to her. She knows what is going on, and she is in control.

We begin to see a pattern here, one that reminds us of something very important. The words of Jesus, "Except a man be born again, he cannot see the kingdom of God," (John 3:3, KJV) begin to make sense to us. Where we once were afraid to be changed, a new exciting perspective begins to emerge. To be born again is to awaken to the comforting arms of the loving Heavenly Father. The fearful unknown to us is known to him that our hearts "might be comforted, being knit together in love, and unto all riches of the full assurance of understanding, to the acknowledgement of the mystery of God . . . In whom are hid all the treasures of wisdom and knowledge" (Col. 2:2, KJV). While we remain too young in Christ to have many proven experiences of His help, He fills our reborn hearts with that same trust in His love that the newborn baby feels with the mother.

God does not have to give us a reason for anything He says, but He does give us enough light to see the next step, which is all we need. In the physical world, it is normal for the newborn to grow. If you ask a new mother how her baby is doing, you get a glowing report of the child's increase in weight and height, along with all kinds of incidental data about sleeping habits, cutting teeth, and recognition of certain people. Are we to assume that God is less pleased with advancement in our spiritual growth and experience?

I would think the saddest parents in the world would be those whose baby never changes after birth, never growing, never learning, never making any sort of progress at all. It is normal to grow physically. Spiritual growth is also normal. Some parents encourage physical growth and ignore the need for spiritual growth. But we are not asked to place one area of growth above the other. Our bodies are sacred gifts from God, for which we are accountable to keep as healthy as possible. The Christian's body is "a living sacrifice, holy, acceptable to God." The apostle John wrote to Gaius, "I pray that you may prosper in all things and be in health, just as your soul prospers" (3 John 2).

Our concern about the body's well-being comes naturally. Jesus emphasized the importance of physical needs when he rebuked those did not give to the hungry, the sick, and the imprisoned. Self-preservation is humanity's strongest natural instinct. Christianity recognizes this, but it insists that we go further. Followers of Christ are to be good Samaritans and thus demonstrate their Christian faith. When Jesus was asked by the Pharisees, "Which is the great commandment in the law?" He told them without hesitation that to love God comes first, but with His next words, he laid down the measuring rod. We prove that we have given God first place in our hearts by our concern for others. "You shall love your neighbor as yourself" (Matt. 22:39). When Jesus was eating His last supper with the disciples, He told them all the significant truths of His purpose on earth. He gave them a clear-cut rule by which believers are distinguished from all others. "By this all will know that you are My disciples, if you have love for one another" (John 13:35).

Christians in any age must look for no other foundation than the one about which Paul testified when he wrote, "For other foundation can no man lay than that is laid, which is Jesus Christ" (1 Cor. 3:11, KJV). Today we look for the quickest ways to do everything! If we are to share the good news of Christ with others, we must first get their attention. We must work to ease, if not end, people's hunger, pain, and loneliness. As Jesus underlined, we must treat the outward, reachable needs before trying to heal the deeper, hidden needs. Even then, there is no guarantee that they will be ready to hear and respond to our "good news."

There must be a hungering and thirsting for the good news before there is belief. In the Beatitudes Jesus said, "Blessed are they which do hunger and thirst after righteousness: for they shall be filled." The "filling" happens after the hungering and thirsting. A friend who disliked to cook once said to me, "Don't bring me your new recipes to try. I only cook because it gets to be time for dinner, and everyone comes in hungry!" Our needs usually cause our actions.

The need we see in the lives of others stirs us to reach out and help. Humanity's deepest need can only be met by Christ Himself, and as we have opportunity to meet other needs, all of us can point the way to Christ.

2
Related in Christ

They shall ask the way to Zion,
With their faces toward it, saying,
"Come and let us join ourselves to the Lord
In a perpetual covenant
That will not be forgotten" (Jer. 50:5).

If asked to explain with one word what life is all about, I would say, *relationships.* That first bond between one person and another begins when the tiny baby is held in the arms of the mother or father. Throughout our lives, all we ever really know of others is in how they relate to us. Hearsay can be very misleading.

The first time my husband took me out, he was careful to explain to me that he was "putting his best foot forward," that he was showing me his good side. What that told me was that he considered me important enough to want me to think well of him. That flattered me! In the time we spent together afterward, he confessed to having a great many faults. I took this as an indication of his honesty. As the relationship developed, I learned that opinions of him by others did not always agree with what I saw in him. And now, after many years with him, it still holds true. Our interaction determines the relationship, not what we may or may not know about each other.

The moods of all of us are directly affected by the reactions of others! Cause and effect are never more related than in human association. Often disagreements between individuals are a result of unfairness, either real or imagined. In theory, we accept this, but when it is my relationship with another that is at stake, how do I deal with it? That depends upon what I want the end result to be. And even that will depend upon what the disagreement is about. If it is an issue that has no moral influence, then pressure on me to "be right" is considerably reduced. We often attempt by argument to prove ourselves right, only to learn that we have lost far more than we gained.

When two people come in conflict with each other, a little warning bell goes off within; this is our first alert notice. It is telling us that it is time to stop and think: *Where am I now, where is this tack taking me, and is that where I want to be?* Obviously, if I want a close relationship with the person involved, I must be very careful. If I really care how that person feels about me, I will avoid character assassination, even by innuendo. Somehow, an argument over facts is a lot easier forgiven and forgotten than one about motives. The more complex our motives, the more protective we usually become of them. And, in anger we are most likely to ignore that little warning bell, which is reason enough to commit Proverbs 14:17 to memory:

> He who is quick-tempered acts foolishly,
> And a man of wicked intentions is hated.

Anger's caustic effect on friendship is like pouring lye water on your prize plants. The plants may be sturdy enough to withstand a few dousings; but under constant drenching, they will wither and die. If you have ever destroyed a friendship in this manner, you know how devastating it can be to you, but you can never estimate the damage to your victim. The times we find

hardest to forget, and rightly so, are those when we intentional-
ly hurt someone with a cutting remark. This turns a simple
difference of opinion into open warfare against the person. The
depressing guilt of just a few such occasions is painful enough
to cause us to put a leash on our tempers. It is important that
we take a close look at how we get along with people because
there is no other single form of evidence that speaks so loudly
about how we relate to God. The impact of our love upon the
lives we touch can be great if it is founded in a mature love of
God that sees Him as both the origin and the object of all love.
To experience such love is to realize that in giving it to all others
we are giving back to God an ever-increasing adoration, which
is the highest form of worship we can hope to offer.

It seems odd that the beginning of a relationship with God is
suggested by a glimpse of its ultimate fullness, but that is usually
the way it happens. We first become conscious of God as we
observe others worshiping Him. Introduced in this normal way,
the idea of God is accepted long before we are prepared to
accept Him personally. With this in mind, can you not see the
tremendous importance of the worshiper? At this point, the
worshiper stands as a guide, pointing the way. What a responsibility one has who has caught the attention of the novice. "If the
trumpet give an uncertain sound, who shall prepare himself to
the battle?" (1 Cor. 14:8, KJV). Throughout history, the trumpet
has been used to announce pertinent decisions of war. In the
heat of battle, the various orders of the commander in charge
were communicated by the arrangement of notes to form a set
musical score for each major dictate. If the trumpeter garbled
his notes, imagine the ensuing chaos! "So likewise you, unless
you utter by the tongue words easy to understand, how will it
be known what is spoken? For you will be speaking into the air"
(v. 9).

The Lord told many parables about ordinary happenings to

show people extraordinary spiritual truths that would have been hard for them to understand otherwise. The sum and substance of these are just as valuable to us today. We do not need new, undiscovered facts or even brilliant, intellectual thoughts. We do need the simple truths of God, wisely applied to our lives. Who could read the parable of the lost sheep without realizing the great sense of bereavement and sorrow experienced by the shepherd? Even the ninety-nine sheep he still had could not make him forget his love for that one which was lost. When he finally found it, he was so happy that he invited all the neighbors in for a celebration. Because of its conclusion, I get excited about that story every time I read it.

"Likewise joy shall be in heaven over one sinner that repenteth, more than over ninety-nine just persons, which need no repentance" (Luke 15:7, KJV). That tells me that I am of inestimable worth to my Heavenly Father; that He loves me so much that to be separated from me for any reason, grieves Him. To look at our relationship to God from that end is a reversal of our usual way of seeing everything from our end and sheds more light on the matter. I can no longer think and act contrary to Him while telling myself that it concerns only me. I can no longer ignore the fact that I am hurting the one who loves me not only more than all others but more than any other can.

We all know that we become more compatible with others when we see things from their point of view; it is an automatic result. To do this, we first must care enough to take the position. When our hearts have become involved enough to engage our minds, our attitude of concern makes an impact.

Martina, a young mother with a handicapped child, was a case in point. Martina worked as a waitress in order to send her child to a good training school and to give him little luxuries. Sadly the crippled son was only a part of Martina's problem. She was married to an overbearing, abusive man; and she was so difficult to get along with that others dreaded to work with her. Customers preferred not to sit at her tables because of her resentful manner. Changing places of employment made little difference until one day a fellow worker rose to the challenge. Fully aware that it would take much patience, Lena decided to become Martina's friend if it killed her. It didn't; though there were times when she could have cheerfully choked Martina.

Little by little, Lena began to see beneath the bitterness to the inside of Martina. The tender devotion to her child, never showing the slightest impatience, was beautiful to watch and gave Lena new insight into the complex young woman who could show such compassion for the imperfect. Little by little, Lena began to understand the hurt that engulfed Martina every time she saw a healthy child and the vindictive feelings she experienced when others brushed aside her boy. Lena began to actually love Martina and her son, becoming protective to the point of often defending her to others. The outcome, not unexpected, was that Martina's attitude toward others softened. To be loved unexpectedly, for no apparent reason, was just the encouragement she needed.

It would be difficult to say who benefitted most from all this. I think I would choose Lena. It was wonderful for Martina to finally have a friend who understood and cared for her, and all those who worked with her must have enjoyed the results. But think what Lena got out of it. Because she disciplined herself to carefully cultivate serenity, she developed patience. This great attribute teaches us more about life in five minutes than many of us learn in a lifetime without it. "For ye have need of patience, that, after ye have done the will of God, you might receive the promise" (Heb. 10:36, KJV). The promise was made by Christ himself, when he said, "In your patience possess your souls" (Luke 21:19).

Recognition of her motive for helping Martina was a big step in Lena's own spiritual growth. To declare our motives for doing anything gives us clearer objectives. There were times when Martina's crass grating on her sensibilities would have caused Lena to give up in disgust had she not committed herself to "helping Martina." Any time we come in conflict with another, it is a good idea to remind ourselves of what we are doing there, of what our purpose really is. If it is to help someone, we find a way to overcome our own injured feelings so we can speak softly in genuine concern for them.

Lena gained many blessings from her friendship with Martina, but her crowning advantage was a closer relationship with God. She would be the first to admit that without Him it would never have worked.

Human relationships consist of give and take, but a perfect balance is never struck. One will always give or take a little more than the other. The key to peace in the heart is found in our proper handling of that word, *more.* Try to be the one willing to give more of life's good—and if a little of the bad must be swallowed, always be the one who will take more of that!

3
Life's Alternatives

See, I have set before you today life and good, death and evil, in that I command you today to love the Lord your God, to walk in His ways, and to keep His commandments, His statutes, and His judgments, that you may live and multiply; and the Lord your God will bless you in the land you go to possess (Deut. 30:15-16).

In the familiar answer of the octogenarian who was asked how he liked being old, there is a bit of wisdom as well as wit. "I enjoy it," he said, "especially when I consider my alternative." The situations we complain about in some cases would receive a lot less protest if we took a long hard look at our alternatives. We are not talking here about *the* alternatives, but *our* alternatives; not in every situation are all possibilities open to us. The octogenarian would likely choose to be young were that option open to him, but realistically it is impossible. The principal reason we refuse to look at reality in every instance is because it is so painful to be honest with ourselves; and that is what reality is—honesty.

From its inception, life is a continuing series of either/or situations. A friend once said to me that his life would run smoothly if he didn't have so many decisions to make. Who would want such a life? There must be scores of "soap operas" on television, but only one of them appeals to me. I do not know when it began, but for twenty years I have seen these same characters struggling along under the burden of their foolish decisions. I have missed episodes for months at a time, only to return and find them embroiled in the same old problems. How long do you think they would hold an audience if they just sat around drinking tea day after day while they discussed the weather? Even in contrived situations, life is more interesting when there are decisions to be made.

The necessity of decisions, and our freedom to make them, lifts us out of mechanical existence into rich experiences requiring energy and imagination. Most of our decisions are not important in the sense that they determine life or death, but almost all of them will affect our futures.

Decisive people attract. We may label them "opinionated" and "bullheaded," but we recognize them as the movers! They get things done. All of those who seem so sure of themselves have one thing in common with the undecided. They know no more about the right thing to do in every circumstance than you or I do. There are very few times when we can know all the facts concerning the past or present of every issue in question, and we can only guess at the future. That limits all of us in our judgment of the outcome. This inability to know in advance how things will come out is one of God's great blessings to us. If we are not absolutely sure where we are going, we will stay closer to our guide.

Can you imagine the frustration of going on a trip in a foreign country with a guide who does not speak your language? A few years ago, I was sight-seeing in Europe with my husband and young daughter. The guide on our bus would first tell the pertinent facts in French, then English. At each point of interest, I eagerly waited for her English narrative. My husband, impatient to get on with it, finally said to me in exasperation, "I wish these people would learn to talk!" His remark became an amusing, little private joke, but it opens up a much overlooked truth. The only way we will ever understand God's word to us is to learn His language.

Jesus told the Galileans that they expected to see signs and wonders before they would believe. Modern people are no different. Have you ever made such a blunder that you foolishly wished you could suddenly become invisible? I have—and that is just about as sensible as wanting God to give us a sign every time we have a decision to make! We all know people whose base of decision is the table of astrological calculations. I suppose if one really wants to believe that Jupiter or Orion or the Big Dipper is pulling the strings of his life, there is nothing to do but let him continue to try bringing enough events into line to validate his belief. God did not equip us to read the future. According to God's teachings, we are to know Him as well as is humanly possible through prayer and His written Word. Using the wisdom He gives us, we are to sort it all out as well as we can. We are still going to make mistakes. We should not let that scare us—when our motives are right. When we have done all we can to bring all the known facts into line with what we sincerely believe to be wise, though we may be proven wrong, God is still with us! As long as we walk with Him, there can be no dead-end streets for us.

Man has always sought freedom. Having found it, some have realized its benefits to such extent as to unselfishly aspire to it for others. In our world, we think of freedom as good and slavery as evil. The precept of slavery opposes all that we see as good in freedom. But sometimes something has looked good while masking a hidden evil, and occasionally what appears to be bad has much potential good to be uncovered. The rationale of this is deduced from our own experience of faith.

In its beginning, our trusting God takes us only far enough to assure us of heaven. To be freed from the consequences of our sins without becoming completely subjugated is our unspoken goal, for we are repulsed by the idea of slavery to anyone. As we progress in spiritual development, our eyes are opened to the bondage hidden within the freedom to obey our sinful natures. The free sinful nature will never be able to consistently honor God. But when it is brought into subjection to Him, bound by His love to conform to His will, we are ready to throw off the shackles that bind us. The truth is, every life serves something or someone. Our choice determines whether the cruelty of Satan's chains will bind us or the gentle cords of God:

> I drew them with gentle cords,
> With bands of love,
> And I was to them as those who take the yoke from their
>   neck.
> I stooped and fed them (Hos. 11:4).

Sin is a ruthless master. Our alternative is the position stated in Romans 6:22: "But now having been set free from sin, and having become slaves of God, you have your fruit to holiness, and the end, everlasting life." Can you read this statement of fact and keep your feet on the ground?

When we set our souls to honor God, even our weaknesses and mistakes cannot overturn the promise, "for those who honor Me I will honor." In choosing our alternatives, we are wise to keep reminding ourselves that no one can have it both ways. We will either live out God's will for our time on earth or not. That *not* is a lot more significant than we might think. It contains a broader scope than its simple refusal implies. In London, I had asked my family to ride the subway with me to Hyde Park. They reluctantly agreed but must have thought it was still open to discussion. When the cars stopped and the doors swung open, they just stood there. The doors clanged shut, and the cars went whizzing down the tracks before I could activate my southern drawl to say a word! While we stood there trying to make up our minds what to do, the decision was taken away from us by the subway train's departure. As long as we put off making up our minds to gain Christ for ourselves, our lives remain as adrift as if we rejected Him with an emphatic no!

4
Singleness of Purpose

Brethren, I count not myself to have apprehended: but this one thing I do, forgetting those things which are behind, and reaching forth unto those things which are before, I press toward the mark for the prize of the high calling of God in Christ Jesus (Phil. 3:13-14, KJV).

Luke 10 gives a short but comprehensive account of a visit Jesus made to the home of Martha and Mary. That passage of Scripture has received its fair share of attention, particularly from women who are sincerely seeking to serve God. This incident, taken apart from all that precedes it, seems to stand alone. To read it by itself, takes away none of its value of teaching. But when we do reach back and read how Jesus first sent out seventy of His followers to minister and to teach and see His joy in their success, our eyes are opened to what is most important in life. Later in Luke 10, Jesus interpreted for the lawyer what it means to love God and our neighbor, making us look beyond the small-world boundaries we set for ourselves.

Jesus sent the seventy to do the same things He came to do. He sent them out with prayer. Wherever we go, praying should be a part of our preparation. Our success depends on it.

Jesus reminded His workers that the harvest was ready. If there are no laborers to harvest the wheat or corn, ripe and waiting to be gathered, it is soon wasted. If we know Jesus at all, we immediately see that His first concern is to save people. His instructions were, "Say unto them, The kingdom of God is come nigh to you" (Luke 10:9, KJV).

As we begin to understand the nature of Jesus, we are better able to see what He was trying to show Martha. Our first impulse is to defend her. We empathize that, after all the work she was doing to make Him more comfortable, Jesus scolded her. Since He had to do it—and if we study this carefully, we can see the necessity of it—we have to like the way He did it! When we are wrong and someone has to correct, how nice it would be to have it so gently done. "Martha, Martha, you are worried and troubled about many things. But one thing is needed" (vv. 41-42).

Looking back over this story, we are reassured that the judgment of Christ is always just. Martha admitted that Mary stopped helping to listen to Jesus. There are never enough Marys in the world: those who will work but know when to stop and wait before the Lord. Those who "rest in the Lord, and wait patiently for him: fret not" themselves over the things beyond their control. Jesus seemed to be correcting Martha more for her attitude than for what she was doing. Are there not far too many of us rushing about with troubled spirits and irritated manners? Rather than see that the real problem is our attitude, we try to lay the blame on others.

Had Martha taken the time to think, she surely would have realized what was important to Jesus. Just as we do when we spend time with Him and hear Him. When we store up His Word and stay close to Him, that same supportive statement He made about Mary becomes our promise. "Mary has chosen that good part, which will not be taken away from her" (v. 42).

If I seem to belabor this story, it is because its precept is the foundation for choosing our course of action for every day we live. Jesus and His companions would have been as well off with less lavish attention to the serving, but Martha took on an enormous handicap by denying herself the joy of Jesus' presence.

"That I may know him" was Paul's aim in his singleness of purpose. "[This] one thing," Jesus said, "is needed." To truly know Jesus is the zenith of knowledge. A lifetime is not enough to complete this great endeavor. We have caught a little of Paul's spirit when we begin to feel his excitement in it. Every day becomes for us a day for the infinite surprise. "This is the day which the Lord has made; We will rejoice and be glad in it," is to us as it was for the psalmist, *de integro Dei gratia:* a new start by the grace of God! To have a fresh beginning, leaving mistakes and heartaches of yesterday behind, is to open a door into unlimited possibilities.

> As it is written:
> Eye has not seen, nor ear heard,
> Nor have entered into the heart of man
> The things which God has prepared for
>   those who love Him   (1 Cor. 2:9).

To know Jesus by knowing Jesus is a paradox, but what matters is that in practice, it works. To have Christ living in us is to have, also, His possibilities.

All of us at times have put ourselves on the spot by stating one of our own moral principles, then finding ourselves in the position of having to live up to it. My grandfather had a phrase for that situation: "Put your money where your mouth is." We have heard it expressed in countless ways; but however the point is made, we know that we are obligated to do what we say; our integrity demands it! God is faithful. His Word declares, "if any provides not for his own, and specially for those of his own house, he hath denied the faith, and is worse than an infidel" (1 Tim. 5:8, KJV). Born of the Spirit, believing that Christ died on the cross to pay the penalty for my sins, and accepting Him as resurrected Lord of my life, I have obediently followed Him in baptism. Does this not make me a member of His household? Then how could He possibly fail to provide my needs without retracting His own promise?

To believe in the all-inclusive, incomprehensible love of God is the single most difficult thing in the world. Because there has to be a reason why so few seem to trust as the Bible tells us to, we try by reasoning to define and correct the perplexity. A small child follows a parent around with perfect peace of mind, never for a moment doubting that parental love. This suggests to us that when Jesus said, "Whosoever shall not receive the kingdom of God as a little child shall in no wise enter therein," He meant for us to accept in simple trust what He gives. We must receive God's love as humbly as a child, without any proud pretense that we can earn it. Our Father's kingdom can be inherited, but it cannot be bought!

The child who expects the parent's love does so because that is what she has come to know. It is the nature of the parent she has learned to trust, not her own worth. Whatever the parent is to any other: teacher, lawyer, judge, doctor, or policeman, he or she is still Father or Mother to that child. Our Heavenly Father is known by many names but always, preceding every name, He is our own personal loving, compassionate Father. He cares for us in ways beyond the reaches of human imagining. How can we possibly doubt such a father?

My youngest daughter was only two years old when her father died. The other children were old enough to remember their loving dad, but Kathy grew up without any firsthand understanding of what she was missing. When she was eleven, I remarried. For Kathy, it was like being born again into a new life. Funny, isn't it, that our whole perspective can be changed by the filling of emptiness in our hearts? Because she needed a loving father, God created in my husband's heart the need for just such a young daughter as Kathy. From the beginning, the rapport between them was beautiful to see. That "spirit of adoption" spoken of in the eighth chapter of Romans became a reality in the relationship. It could never have happened without a daily association in which Kathy experienced the concern and tenderness of a father's love.

It never seems to cross our minds that there is more to a relationship with our Heavenly Father than, "Help me, Lord, I am in trouble," or "I really need this, Father, and I need it now!" These cries are, of course, a part of the relationship and are always heard and responded to, according to our need. The response is not always in keeping with our plans, but we can count on it being the best thing for us.

I find it very frustrating to try to please someone I care about when I cannot find out what it is they want from me. The harder I try, the more I seem to irritate. We do not have that problem with God. His Word is open to us. His very nature is there for us to study and experience.

No wonder Christians who have so little to do with God are not finding much to cheer about. The cheering starts when someone is winning! At a sporting event, when one side or the other takes the lead, spectators become excited. When our purpose is to know Christ, "and the power of his resurrection," even the smallest gain kindles a thrill of elation in living. To be always pressing forward toward "the prize of the high calling of God in Christ Jesus" is vital! To set this as our single purpose is to include every worthwhile goal.

5
The Seekers

Ask, and it will be given to you; seek, and you will find; knock,
and it will be opened to you (Matt. 7:7).

My husband is constantly losing something that he needs
around the house—at least he convinces me that he needs it. I
am sure my habit of wanting to know all about it before I help
him look for it is somewhat irritating. But before I start searching, I want to be sure of recognizing what I am searching for.

The world is full of seekers. What percentage of these do you
suppose would recognize what they are seeking if they found
it?

They may be somewhat like the young man who admired
beauty so much that he insisted on spending his time in the
company of only the very attractive. He dated one beautiful girl
after another with the idea that one day he would find such
perfection of form and feature that he would fall in love forever.
An accident at the construction site where he worked blinded
him, forcing his life in a different direction. In a rehabilitation
school, he met a young lady whose job was to help the handicapped adjust to their limitations. She often read to the young
man. As time went by, he learned that she spent all her spare
time and means in service to others. Her quick mind and blithe

spirit drew him, as it did others, out of their darkness into her sunlight.

The relationship between the blind young man and the lovely Christian girl deepened until one day he could no longer hide his love for her. Holding her close, he told her how he felt and why. He said, "All my life I promised myself that I would marry the prettiest girl in the world, and nothing is changed. My fingers on your face tell me what beautiful features are there."

With her tears dripping onto his hands, she answered, "If you could see, you would know how wrong you are. Those 'beautiful features' are obscured by a livid birthmark covering my entire face." The man had found the true beauty he was seeking, but without his lost eyesight, he would never have recognized her.

If we look up the word *seek* in the dictionary, we will see that it means to go in search of, to strive for. This implies action of some sort. But it is also true that we need to first get a mental picture of what we want. Shakespeare's idea, "Assume a virtue, if you have it not," works for all to a point, but the Christian has an added advantage. Anyone can create in his mind an image of the person he wants to be, but no matter how hard he tries, the day will come when the bull will break through the fence. Just when he is leaving for an important appointment, someone will have left the gas tank on empty, and he will discover grease on his coat sleeve. Right away, his "feet of clay" take over.

Paul must have had just such a day when he cried, "O wretched man that I am! Who will deliver me from this body of death?" We can identify with his dilemma, "For the good that I will to do, I do not do; but the evil I will not to do, that I practice." Paul's cry is also our cry. It is here that Christians have an advantage. To the question of who will deliver us, our reply is the same as Paul's: "I thank God—through Jesus Christ our Lord! So then, with the mind I myself serve the law of God, but with the flesh the law of sin" (see Rom. 7:19,24-25).

If this seems to offer an excuse for sin, it in no way does. It does explain that there is always conflict between God's grace and Satan's evil. To accept what God, through the death of Christ on the cross, did for us is enough to discover sin and burden us with it, but only walking with Christ will free us from it. "He who calls you is faithful, who also will do it" (1 Thess. 5:24). What He will do is "sanctify you completely; [that] your whole spirit, soul, and body be preserved blameless at the coming of our Lord Jesus Christ" (v. 23).

To seek happiness is not selfish or wrong. To seek it as an entity, without regard for its consequence to others, is not only selfish and wrong but foolish as well. Somehow, common sense seems to fly out the window when people consider spiritual matters. Those laws God set in motion at creation are in effect here. This is just another order of things that we attempt to reverse. Jesus came to live among men as a man, to heal and to teach and to save. His purpose, as He stated it, was "that they might have life, and that they might have it more abundantly" (John 10:10, KJV). After He is our Lord comes the abundance, not before! He could not put it any clearer than this: "Your heavenly Father knows that you need all these things. But seek first the kingdom of God and His righteousness, and all these things shall be added to you" (Matt. 6:32-33).

We might be happy with just a few of "these things" but Jesus said we could have them all. However, He did not agree with us on how to get them. Jesus' method sounds unorthodox to those whose shrine is expediency. But those who will think it through know that happiness which is dependent upon fleeting emotion can disappear as quickly as the emotion it is tied to. To seek happiness as a goal is to choose the most impossible one to reach, for it is obvious to the truly happy that the only source is God, "for every good gift and every perfect gift is from above, and cometh down from the Father" (Jas. 1:17, KJV). Seek, then,

the source because happiness is a natural by-product that blos-
soms when we seek God and His righteousness as our worthy
goal.

People sometimes confuse happiness with pleasure. I take
great pleasure in the Kansas City Chiefs knocking off an oppos-
ing football team, but it has nothing to do with my lasting
happiness.

There is a law of demand and supply that works spiritually as
surely as the recognized economic principle. Until we put it
into practice, we deny ourselves the power of obtaining what
our Father stands ready to give. Our need impels our Lord's
supplying. Remember His statement in the Sermon on the
Mount:

> Blessed are those who hunger and
>   thirst for righteousness,
> For they shall be filled (Matt. 5:6).

The woman of Zarephath who used her last handful of meal
and her last bit of oil to make bread to feed Elijah, never had
to worry again about starving. "And the barrel of meal wasted
not, neither did the cruse of oil fail, according to the word of
the Lord, which he spake by Elijah" (1 Kings 17:16, KJV). Her
hospitable act did not inspire the reward; she had already told
Elijah of her intention to use the meal and oil to feed her son.
God rewarded her obedience to His command. Her destitute
condition made her obedience even more impressive.

When reading God's Word, we need to stop and try to think
through to a logical reason for God's actions. This must be what
the psalmist had in mind when he spoke of the happiness to be
found by the one who doesn't walk in the counsel of the ungodly
nor waste his time with the skeptics: "But his delight is in the
law of the Lord; and in his law doth he meditate day and night"
(Ps. 1:2, KJV). To meditate in God's law is to see truths we might

otherwise overlook. God had promised to feed Elijah. He could have as easily sent him to someone with plenty instead of to a starving widow. When we thoughtfully consider God's ways, we can remember many desperate occasions when help came just in time. In most of these times, it is amazing how often the lives of others were involved. In our simple trust, it is easy to overlook the fact that we are a part of something much greater in God's plan than what we can immediately see. In His omniscience, He sees us all as related, and He works things out accordingly. In meeting Elijah's need, God reached out to include the widow and her son.

Most of us think we know what our priority in life is. But there also are many who would be hard pressed to say, for they have never bothered to set for themselves a clear goal. A great fault in this inability to set definite goals is scattered thought. Divided resources cannot effect cumulative positive action. How many passing thoughts flicker through the mind and are lost forever? To bring our minds into correlation with the Spirit's power requires sustained thought, producing a projected mental picture. True meditation is probing all the possibilities in a contemplative way.

If my priority is to find what is conducive to happiness, it will become necessary for me to sacrifice a few momentary pleasures along the way. And it will be better accomplished if I have laid the proper groundwork: thought patterns that spring into action at the first sign of trouble.

> Your word I have hidden in my heart,
> That I might not sin against You (Ps. 119:1).

With God's Word properly applied for every situation, we are connecting our resources to a phenomenal power that causes miraculous things to happen. To find for ourselves the highest good, we must follow Paul's instructions to the Philippians:

Finally, brethren, whatever things are true, whatever things are
noble, whatever things are just, whatever things are pure, whatever things are lovely, whatever things are of good report, if
there is any virtue and if there is anything praiseworthy—meditate on these things (4:8).

During a fragment of my growing up years, we lived in a part
of Arkansas that was extremely rocky and hilly. As I remember
it, those rocks were better for breaking hoe handles and backs
than for growing corn and cotton, but the younger generation
found a way to enjoy the rough terrain when the work ended.
The rocky cliffs near by, especially the almost vertical ones,
were an exciting challenge to the strength and daring of my
brother and our cousin, along with a friend from across the
hollow. The first time I was allowed to tag along the prospect
of scaling the Matterhorn could not have been more exciting.
We all carefully avoided mentioning to my mother that instead
of watching from below as usual, her dainty little girl was making her first mountain climb. By the time the day ended, if I
knew no more about mountain climbing than before, I was
certainly enlightened on the advisability of sticking to pursuits
more in keeping with my talents. The skinned and bruised
elbows and knees healed, and the sting of my mother's scolding
eased. But I can still recall the panic of looking down from the
dizzying height while clinging to a tiny bush growing out of the
rocky face of that cliff. In the years since, I have often thought
of that experience because of its threat to me. In that moment
of dangling from a sapling, with my hands smarting from scrat-
ches, I was frightened. The shouts of encouragement from the
anxious faces peering down from the ledge at the top were too
far away to be of immediate help.

Have you come to such a time in life? If not, you will. Sooner
or later, that stick you were braced against will give way. Those

you placed your trust in for all things will fall, revealing a human frailty. As you grope for a solid foothold, the hands of those who would help you cannot quite reach. It is then that God's voice will sound your depths. It is then that you will know for certain:

> The Lord's hand is not shortened,
> That it cannot save;
> Nor His ear heavy,
> That it cannot hear (Isa. 59:1).

Were I to return today to look at that hill I climbed, I am sure it would not seem as dangerous. When the storms of life are past and God has brought us safely through, it is not unusual for us to look back on the receding darkness as a time that made us wiser and better.

In public places, especially those where people must wait, such as airports and bus stations, I make a game of looking at faces and using my imagination about them. This may make the waiting time less boring, but sadly, I know nothing of what those people really are like. Even more sad is the fact that many of them don't know either.

The game I play is a lot like the one they play every day. The attractive young girl is an undiscovered star with fame and fortune waiting at the next airport. The tight-faced salesman is living beyond his means because the image he has manufactured for himself is based on his conviction that he deserves the best. The housewife is having a lot of trouble adjusting to a continuing expectation of more than she finds possible to give. They are all hung up on the snag Paul warned against in Romans 12:3: "For I say, through the grace given unto me, to every man that is among you, not to think of himself more highly than he ought to think; but to think soberly, according as God hath dealt to every man the measure of faith" (KJV).

Some of our deepest troubles are rooted in pride. Jesus never wantonly hurt any person or angrily insisted upon his rights no matter what opposition he encountered. If we let nothing be done through selfish ambition or conceit but in lowliness of mind esteem others better than ourselves (see Phil. 2:3), the abrasiveness in our relationships with all others will be smoothed.

Children are masters at playacting. Cops and robbers, cowboys and Indians, playing house—are all acted out in a very real way. But it doesn't really change anyone. Children are more perceptive than some adults; for when the game ends, children know it. They knew all along that they were only pretending. "If anyone thinks himself to be something when he is nothing, he deceives himself" (Gal. 6:3). If we say we are Christians, if we attend the various churches and afterwards go out to our life pursuits in the same old manner, what has changed?

A few years ago, my daughter, Sandra, and I left our families behind and went on a vacation trip to Hawaii. She, an avid shopper, bought all kinds of trinkets, including an unusual Japanese lantern which stated in English on the box that the instructions were inside. I noticed that she very carefully examined the contents of the box before putting it away, but she made no comment. Toward the end of our stay, it was obvious that she was experiencing the pangs of homesickness. Late one afternoon we were lying across our beds talking when I heard sounds of ukuleles outside. Jumping up to look out of the window, I said, "Let's go, Sandy! They are playing their music, and there is a big buffet spread down by the pool." She looked wearily at me and said in disgust, "Mother, I am tired of their music, I don't like their food, and furthermore, I have bought a lantern with Japanese instructions." The Bible does not contain instructions for one group to the exclusion of others, for there is no partiality with God. If we are vague in our minds about the clear mandates from God, it is not the fault of the Bible. The confusion we feel is not because God has failed to make clear the way of seeking Him. It is because we refuse to rid ourselves of the carnal nature of self. "Seek the Lord while He may be found, Call upon Him while He is near" is His sure Word to us, whoever we are.

6
If God Be God

And Elijah came to all the people, and said, "How long will you falter between two opinions? If the Lord is God, follow Him; but if Baal, then follow him." But the people answered him not a word (1 Kings 18:21).

Knowing God's Word on a given subject before attempting to understand the principles of His work with that subject is important. If God is the omnipotent "I Am" of all things, then we should stand our ground for Him. If, like the Israelites of Elijah's day, we have doubts about it, then like them, maybe we have nothing to say. God's principles work because they are altogether true and right, and any effort of ours to reverse the order of this is to undermine the basic tenet of our faith. To think His principles true because we sometimes see them work is to dilute our faith and delude ourselves. If God is not who He says He is, then He is not worth considering, for, at best, His promises would be no better than those of any unreliable person. How long has it been since you had a real concrete, visible answer to a specific prayer? A week, a month, a year? For some, a decade might be more accurate. If God is who He says He is, you can have all that He has promised.

To believe that God is, then to begin doubting the Word that supports His existence, is no better than to have a hypothetical house with hypothetical parents living in it; you can never experience the security of the home, and you can never know the love of the parents. You may long for it and dream of one day possessing such faith, but until you take the initiative of opening your heart and walking into it, leaving all else, it will not become your reality. How can a completely spiritual Someone ever be totally reconciled to a worldly being who is a little bit spiritual only part of the time? It can never be! We can simulate a real "oneness" with church activities, social work, and donations to worthy causes, but we are only fooling those as gullible as ourselves. We are permitting our "friend Baal" to get away with the lie that God is pleased to have us on our own terms.

God's Word says, "So then, because you are lukewarm, and neither cold nor hot, I will spew you out of My mouth" (Rev. 3:16). A little bit of God is a dangerous thing, dangerous because He will not tolerate it. You won't find much stronger language in the Bible than Exodus 34:14, in which God took upon Himself the name, "Jealous." "For you shall worship no other god, for the Lord whose name is Jealous, is a jealous God." This gives us pause for thought, for most of us know the unpleasant results of a well-founded jealousy. The opposite view gives us a beautiful picture of commitment. When we trust God completely, we can claim the promise He made to Caleb at the entrance of the land of milk and honey: "He shall see it, and to him and his children I am giving the land on which he walked, because he wholly followed the Lord" (Deut. 1:36).

To attempt to control the Holy Spirit is to invite torment, for there can be no peace without surrender. As in Elijah's day, answering God "not a word" is considered an answer, for God's promises are only to those who will trust Him.

> The Lord is good,
> A stronghold in the day of trouble;
> And He knows those who trust in Him (Nah. 1:7).

To trust God is to hold on and not let go, no matter what! Job laid his life on the line with these words: "Though He slay me, yet will I trust Him!" (Job 13:15). He further asked of God:

> Only two things do not do to me:
> ....
> Withdraw You hand far from me,
> And let not the dread of You
> make me afraid (vv. 20-21).

There are times when we can find joy in nothing but God. If we have a strong, working relationship with Him, these times are when our joy in Him is deepest. God's tremendous power is cause for dread to those faraway, but all those who draw close to Him will find Him a familiar and comforting presence.

In trouble, our weakness becomes apparent to us. God always sees where it lies, but until He exposes it, we keep trying to cover it over. Before a psychiatrist can do his work, he must first probe beneath the protective facade of his patient to reach the root of the problem. I am told that often the patient will strenuously resist this, even though he wants to be helped. Human nature throws up this same resistance to God. He, unlike the psychiatrist, does not have to wait for us to stop throwing up smoke screens and get honest with Him in order to know our problem. He knows what is in the heart of all men. He has to make us face in ourselves what he already knew.

At a particular point, we stand alone in the crossroad. If we choose to follow God, we will turn our backs on Baal, for God and Baal do not travel side by side. Baal may try to imitate God's ways in order to get our attention, but he cannot hide his true nature for long. "Beloved, do not believe every spirit, but test

the spirits, whether they are of God; because many false proph-
ets have gone out into the world" (1 John 4:1).

The Book of Numbers presents a graphic example of a false
prophet in the episodes involving Balaam. He was so intent on
self-promotion as a conjurer that he could not see his opportunities to serve the living God. The donkey he rode could discern
the hand of God, though Balaam could not. We marvel at a man
who heard a donkey speak words to him, yet saw nothing abnor-
mal in it; but we are often just as blind to God's providential
hand on our lives. Upon reading this account of Balaam's experience, a friend remarked that if God would just send an angel
to us we would be more easily convinced of His will. I asked,
"Why from an angel's mouth, when we already have God's
direct word to us in the Bible?" His answer expressed a basic
problem. "But that is just a book," he said, "just words." In a few
words, he told why there is so little interest in Scripture searching. If we regard it as a revered, old book that has no application
for today, that is about all the good it will do us. But when we
see the Bible as God's present word to us, its power will invade
our lives! The best book ever written about the Bible can accomplish no more than to point to the Bible's power to change
lives.

Our problems could often be solved if we would just open our
eyes to what causes them. We prefer to deal with spiritual
problems by physical means. We could save time and trouble
by reminding ourselves that the reason for the angel standing
in Balaam's path was Balaam's refusal to obey God. Had he been
spiritually perceptive, Balaam would have seen the angel.

None of us can ignore our responsibility to the lost. We must
care enough to do something, but we ought to use common
sense in determining what to do. There may be times when we
can do no more than Stephen did at the moment of death, when
looking out at his tormentors, he prayed, "Lord, do not charge

them with this sin" (Acts 7:60). That prayer might have been the catalyst that, soon afterward, brought Saul to his knees on the road to Damascus.

There is no use trying to prove God to those who do not believe that He exists. Obviously, if they are of that persuasion, argument is not going to convince them that their needs can be supplied by Someone they consider a nonentity. They have convinced themselves that they are self-sufficient, that their own cleverness can provide for them. In the face of that attitude, we have no recourse but to pray for them, while allowing them to see the truth of Christ reflected in us. God does answer prayer, and "is longsuffering toward us, not willing that any should perish but that all should come to repentance" (2 Pet. 3:9).

No one who has set himself against God is going to have his mind changed by human argument. He makes his choice, and God's judgment is to let him have the consequences of that choice. Our strongest influence can reach just so far; it takes the Creator's power to make a new creature! "If anyone is in Christ, he is a new creation; old things have passed away; behold, all things have become new" (2 Cor. 5:17).

7
Had It Not Been for Jesus

But now in Christ Jesus you who once were far off have been made near by the blood of Christ (Eph. 2:13).

He who sees Me sees Him who sent Me (John 12:45).

Christ, living among men, revealed that in addition to the power and intellect of the Creator there is a personality to whom we can respond. "The only begotten Son, who is in the bosom of the Father, He has declared Him." (John 1:14). In the person of Jesus, we have a threefold look at God as the caring Father, the mediating Savior Son, and the Holy Spirit actually alive in us.

My friend Jamall is an evangelistic concert singer. He sings a very moving song about a place called Calvary and a man named Jesus. Had it not been for Jesus my soul would be lost for eternity. When I listen to this song, the meaning in its words holds such emotional sway over me that I cannot put it out of my mind. Its tender pathos fills me with thoughts of the majestic Eternal Presence becoming flesh to live among us and willingly going to the cross for me. "And the Word became flesh and dwelt among us, and we beheld His glory, the glory as of the only begotten of the Father, full of grace and truth" (John 1:14). The magnificent voice of my friend is the instrument that brings the song to life in stirring simplicity, but the message makes it personal.

No one can visualize the cruelties of the crucifixion without considering Isaiah's prophetic words:

> So His visage was marred more than any man,
> And His form more than the sons of men (52:14).

The effects of man's brutalities were seen on this perfect representative of God's truth and grace and glory. Who can come to the cross and leave without responding to it? The only acceptable response is to embrace it and incorporate it into our lives—refusing to do that is to join those who mocked Him and cast lots for His clothing. Upon what have we placed our values?

Through the mystery of love saving through sacrifice, I can enter into the holy presence of God. "But as many as received Him, to them He gave the right to become children of God, even to those who believe in His name" (John 1:12). On the cross, Jesus cleared me from sin. In the resurrection, He assured my future for eternity. In the simple act of my receiving Him, I became a child of God.

Had Jesus not come to earth, much of what we know about God's nature would have remained unrevealed. When Philip asked Jesus to show them the Father, Jesus acted surprised that His disciples could be so long with Him without knowing Him better. He patiently explained His relationship to the Father, plainly stating, "He who has seen Me has seen the Father" (John 14:9). If we really want to know God, we must literally absorb the nature and teachings of Jesus. In our acceptance of what He did, we receive the nature—His teachings will occupy us as long as we live. The impact of studying Him is no more in what we extract from Him than in what He extracts from us.

We must stop ignoring the basic tenet of Jesus' instruction

that "God is Spirit, and those who worship Him must worship in spirit and truth" (John 4:24). As Christians, our difficulties are not so much in our lack of understanding that the spiritual world is as real as the physical as it is in our neglecting to exercise the spiritual. By ignoring the spiritual, we deny its reality. We do this because we have conditioned ourselves to choose what is seen over the unseen. The fallacy in this is that we make judgments on what we see and not on what is there for us to see if we would open our spiritual eyes.

Though our standing in Christ is secured forever, the state of our spiritual maturity often requires the Father's correction. We need to develop the practice of looking for His hand in every trace of discipline. It is there. Nothing can reach us unless He allows it. In His work of eliminating the habits that do us harm, He may have to lead us through the fire; but "if you endure chastening, God deals with you as with sons; for what son is there whom a father does not chasten?" (Heb. 12:7). He jolts us loose from those characteristics significant to our insecurities so we can develop those characteristics that cannot be jolted.

When we set our hearts on God, to hunger and thirst for His righteousness, He has unlimited resources with which to fill us. If the Bible were our only resource, His Word would be sufficient, but He often uses people and circumstances in conjunction with the Word. A mature, devoted Christian became a friend to a new convert who was still struggling with his old nature. At every opportunity, they discussed their beliefs and the promises of the Bible. The older Christian was a reticent, humble man, more inclined to listen than to speak. The young convert often complained of the conflict within himself and of his clashes with others. Each time, his friend would nod understandingly and say:

> Your word I have hidden in my heart,
> That I might not sin against You (Ps. 119:11).

After this had gone on for a while, in exasperation the younger man exclaimed, "Why do you keep saying that to me? I need some advice to help me control my temper!"

"That is just what I am giving you," his friend answered. "This is God's advice to you, and it is a lot better than mine. If you will listen to these words and do what they tell you, you will see that it works."

When we get the Word in our hearts, we have connected with the power of the Holy Spirit to keep us from sin. One of the most quoted verses in the Scriptures is "As [a man] thinks in his heart, so is he" (Prov. 23:7). It is also one of the least understood. It is not the passing thought but the determination of our hearts that shows what we are. "A good man out of the good treasure of his heart brings forth good; and an evil man out of the evil treasure of his heart brings forth evil. For out of the abundance of the heart his mouth speaks" (Luke 6:45). We go to great lengths to delude ourselves, though we insist we hate deceit. What we actually mean is that we will not tolerate it in others. God feels the same way about dishonesty. It is worth noting that because God is altogether righteous, only He has the right to condemn it. Which He does. "All liars shall have their part in the lake which burns with fire and brimstone, which is the second death" (Rev. 21:8). His position is also clearly stated in Proverbs 6:16-19:

> These six things the Lord hates,
> Yes, seven are an abomination to Him:
> A proud look,
> A lying tongue,
> Hands that shed innocent blood,
> A heart that devises wicked plans,

> Feet that are swift in running to evil,
> A false witness who speaks lies,
> And one who sows discord among the brethren.

Every one of these sins comes straight from the heart.

Being tempted to commit such sins as these given in Proverbs is the very point at which Christ has promised to meet us. He is always there, but we often ignore Christ's presence and stubbornly charge off alone! At the moment of that first flash of anger or that first gossiping slip or that momentary departure from truth, His word in our hearts brought quickly to mind will release all the power of the Holy Spirit to stand with us against our carnal natures. Full power is always available to God's obedient children. The One who blesses is never denied us; but because of disobedience, the blessing often is.

"I will pray the Father, and He will give you another Helper, that He may abide with you forever" (John 14:16). Jesus promised His followers an indwelling Comforter, a Helper at all times, and that is what it means for Him to abide in us. We have so long given the excuse that we cannot possibly keep God's commandments that we have come to believe it; and in this attitude, we allow our feelings to govern our actions. If we can happily accept this in ourselves, we had better go back to the beginning and start over, for something is wrong here. Jesus never spoke anything that was untrue; He never commanded us to do anything that was impossible. He said, "If you keep my commandments, you will abide in My love, just as I have kept My Father's commandments and abide in His love" (John 15:10).

This statement is no cause for confusion as to our salvation. Just as we can be born only once physically, we can be born spiritually only once. After we are born physically, there is no doubt that we are here; our bodily existence is proof. If the spiritual birth is real—if it actually happens—it should be just as visible. The confusion then, is not in our salvation but in our way of life. Our safety is not in danger here; our sanctity is. Before we despair of either, we should prayerfully consider 1 John 3:23: "This is His commandment: that we should believe on the name of His Son Jesus Christ and love one another, as He gave us commandment." This is the love of God working through our faith. It in no way disagrees with the Commandments as given to Moses, for Jesus said, "I did not come to destroy [the law] but to fulfill [it]" (Matt. 5:17). Nothing of God's law was done away with; but through the cross of Christ, it was satisfied. The old covenant was the hope of God's people for centuries. Jesus obtained for us "a better covenant, which was established on better promises" (Heb. 8:6). That better covenant of grace offers us assistance to perform it.

Under God's grace, all His law is fulfilled in the precedent Jesus set. Constant dependancy on Him is assumed as surely as a branch depends on its vine for sustenance. Apart from His constant supplying, there can be no fruitful, satisfying life. In Jesus' simple analogy of the vine and the branches, we see that there is nothing complicated about abiding in Him. It is just a matter of staying connected by allowing no thought or act to remain which will separate us from Him.

Some believers mistake working for Christ with abiding in Him. I have tried it both ways, and the work never prospered until it was a resulting action of the abiding. Did He not say, "Without Me you can do nothing"? That word, *nothing,* is the tip-off to why we sometimes get so little done. The branch is nothing but what the vine puts into it; cut it off and see how much fruit grows! If we could somehow see ourselves as nothing without Him, we would start clearing our hearts of all clutter. Then, He could fill us with His nature.

Had it not been for Jesus, the abundant life would not be

possible for us. "I have come that they may have life, and that they may have it more abundantly" (John 10:10). That was Jesus' stated purpose in coming. If joy is not in us—such joy that it overflows from us—maybe it is because we are trying to live out our own plans in our own ways. We may often plead with God to put His stamp of approval on our plans, forgetting that we are not our own; we are "bought with a price" (1 Cor. 6:20). Selfishness is man's first law of nature; selflessness is God's. We must surrender our self-love before we can have all that abundance of which Jesus spoke.

Life is a constant repetition of cares and pains that in an arbitrary way can sap our strength. "Rejoice in the Lord always. Again I will say, rejoice!" (Phil. 4:4). These words were written by Paul from inside prison walls as testimony that Christian experience is the fire within and not the stirring without.

When the angels delivered that miraculous birth announcement to earth, "Do not be afraid, for behold, I bring you good tidings of great joy which shall be to all people. For there is born to you this day in the city of David a Savior, who is Christ the Lord," they were not just giving out script for a Christmas program. These tidings of great joy are as true today as they were then. He was born our Savior! If He is our Savior, we should start rejoicing that He is!

8
Grace, Grace!

Who are you, O great mountain?
Before Zerubbabel you shall become a plain!
And he shall bring forth the capstone
With shouts of "Grace, grace to it!"
(Zech. 4:7).

Called by His grace; saved by His grace; finding His grace sufficient! These three stages of Christian development lived out are the best explanation we can make visible of the doctrine of grace. After we have experienced the first two stages, we enter into the third: the great thrill of unfolding the secrets of all our tomorrows day-by-day in the presence of Christ. Paul spoke of being called through the grace of Christ, but he also said that we are called into the grace of Christ. This third stage of grace is so incomprehensible in its enormity of purpose that we can only bear it in measure proportionate to our immediate need. Our response determines its ultimate extent.

I grew up in the South near many artesian wells. The clear sparkling water never ceased its flow. The principle of an artesian well is that, once the well is drilled and water is reached, internal pressure brings the water to the surface like a fountain. This is like what Jesus described to the Samaritan woman: "Whoever drinks of the water that I shall give him will never thirst. But the water that I shall give him will become in him a fountain of water springing up into everlasting life" (John 4:14). Jesus was not speaking of a scant trickle, but some believers seem to want just barely enough to save them from death. These never have enough to refresh them in dry, troubled times and are continuously struggling against their embattled deserts. Do you know of a time when God ever gave anything in paltry measure? We will never see that happen. "Command those who are rich in this present age not to be haughty, nor to trust in uncertain riches but in the living God, who gives us richly all things to enjoy" (1 Tim. 6:17).

In previous chapters we have touched on progressive plateaus in our Christian development. The saddest Christian in the world must be the one who has sought to meet all the conditions for this wellspring of living water and somehow missed its overflowing effect in his life. The failure is not so much a lack of willingness to do, as a lack of understanding what to do. We are often deceived into choosing a good thing at the risk of missing the better. Many more are willing to work and pray for blessings from God than are willing to just make the necessary surrender to bring the blessing.

This example may help us to see what is blocking the overflowing fountain of living water. If a man and a woman both agree to marriage, obtain a license, and go through a ceremony, they may enter their home as husband and wife. Suppose after all that, the bride does not surrender herself to the bridegroom, but attempts to manifest the conjugal state in a purely outward manner. She cooks and cleans and manages the budget proficiently. Shouldn't she by rights then experience all the secret joys of a shared intimacy? How could she? Until she is surrendered to the groom in this sacred union, she cannot possibly know its joys.

The surrendered believer has met all the conditions. Not only is he experiencing the joy of Christ in his daily life, but his joy is overflowing into the thirsty lives of those seeking the secret of such a wellspring. Pain and sorrow may often invade this life, but nothing can take away the childlike faith that flows forth in praise to the Father. This grace, once given, is never canceled:

> But He gives more grace. Therefore He says:
> "God resists the proud,
> But gives grace to the humble" (Jas. 4:6)

The Scripture at the beginning of the chapter tells of an angel speaking with Zechariah to let him know that God's work would continue and be completed in spite of "great mountains" that seemed insurmountable. Instead of using visible force, the word to Zerubbabel was

> "Not by might nor by power,
>   but by My Spirit,"
> Says the Lord of hosts (Zech. 4:6)

The Spirit does its work with power but its might is often concealed from the eyes of men. The results are always visible. Under God's grace, our mountains can be reduced to plains. What He begins in us and for us He will continue, for God will never forsake the work He has begun. When everything goes well for us, we feel His love and see His blessings. It is easy then to shout, "Grace, grace!" But when our plans fall through and nothing seems to go right, we forget the very meaning of grace in our fears of the future. We begin to think and act as if God did not know what would happen and might not be prepared to handle it.

When God's unmerited favor was given to us, it was not because we were good or deserving but because Christ is that and more. That is why humility is necessary, putting to death every prideful act of ours. Our only standing is in Christ. To understand this is to begin to understand grace. The hard places along the way, the failures, the hurt, are all necessary to us, "for offenses must come" (Matt. 18:7). Without them, we would never bring ourselves to throwing out the inordinate love of self that clogs the flow of grace. Those who have learned the secret of the fullness of God's grace made their discovery in a gracious welcoming of whatever seemed good to Him to send. And they only learned that secret after they began to see the hand of God in the events involving them, instead of seeing only the hands of others.

If we allow resentment to touch God's dealings with us, our impression on others is one of egoism instead of grace. At all times we are to show others the spirit of Christ. When we lift him Up before others, He truly does draw all people. "And I, if I am lifted up from the earth, will draw all peoples to Myself" (John 12:32). Jesus' words signified the manner in which His life would be given, but they also signified the ultimate glory in His death. Paul's statement that "we glory in tribulations" must also become our truth.

It is impossible to think of grace sufficient to meet every need without considering Paul's "thorn in the flesh," though we are not told its exact nature. Often thrilled by the visions he had received, he was careful to boast of Christ, never himself! "lest I should be exalted above measure by the abundance of the revelations, a thorn in the flesh was given to me, a messenger of Satan to buffet me, lest I be exalted above measure. Concerning this thing I pleaded with the Lord three times that it might depart from me" (2 Cor. 12:7-8). It makes me uncomfortable to think about the hardships Paul endured at the hands of men. He was beaten, stoned, robbed, imprisoned, and often denied life's barest comforts. In all this, he thought himself proof of God's demonstrative love.

Paul's attitude makes us even more uncomfortable; it doesn't take much adversity to discourage most of us. The answer to his plea for healing, "My grace is sufficient for you, for My strength is made perfect in weakness," gave him renewed patience to endure. In another letter, he spoke of that "crown of righteousness which the Lord, the righteous Judge, will give to me on that Day." He must have had a glimpse of that same visionary sight possessed by Isaiah when he cried:

> Those who wait on the Lord
> Shall renew their strength;
> They shall mount up with wings like eagles (40:31)

My children were young when death took their father in a sudden massive heart attack. I have no way of knowing all that was in their hearts, but the devastation was wrenching, from the oldest, a sixteen-year-old son, to the youngest, a two-year-old daughter. I have always believed that the blow was less bitterly absorbed by the thirteen-year-old daughter and the nine-year-old son. I am not saying they did not suffer as deeply, and again, this is only my opinion. I am saying that these two in the middle seemed better equipped to handle their loss. If it is true that they accepted their tragedy with less confusion, I believe it was a result of the grace of God that they were able to appropriate. It was many years before the older son could speak easily of his dad. The trauma for the youngest was most likely rooted in the inability of a two-year-old mentality to comprehend such a loss.

It is difficult even after many years to describe my own feelings in that experience. The suddenness with which I was plunged from the warmth of a satisfying, secure, and still romantic marriage into the hard, cold reality of isolation, was a shock that defies the descriptive powers. If the word *isolation* seems too strong, believe me, it is not. That jolting severance that dispatches one on a one-way journey, sets apart the one left behind as surely as an island is separated from the mainland. Supportiveness from others cushions the blow, but no one can take away the sense of engulfing loneliness.

Surrounded by friends and family, I was caught up in a scene in which everyone reacted in an expected way, bringing their kindness and speaking words of comfort in hushed tones. My own reaction was a calm, moment-to-moment, mechanical response to an unreal force propelling me, as if by maintaining control of myself I could reverse the rushing madness. Inwardly, a seething rebellion against this monstrous outrage drove me to confront the One with all the answers. Acutely aware of my need to seek out God, I pretended drowsiness in order to withdraw from my friends. At last, I was in my bed alone. At that moment all the polite defenses collapsed. In agony my heart cried, "God, I love you and I trust you, but you have placed more confidence in me than I can live up to! You must know this is the one thing I cannot do."

I wish there were words to adequately tell what happened then. A sense of ease and comfort wrapped softly around me, and a lifting sensation went throughout my body. I could actually feel the warmth and strength of being gently held! It was not imagination. Nothing in the years since has been more real, more substantive. My helpless, "I cannot do this," brought an answer that was more felt than heard; but the words were distinct and they were convincing: "You do not have to; I will do it for you." "And the peace of God, which surpasses all understanding" truly does guard the heart and mind of the surrendered believer, for I slept then, soundly and dreamlessly. This is that grace sufficient to meet every need of which Paul spoke.

Truer words were never spoken than those whispered in my heart that night. In the trying times that followed, and there were many, every problem was met, every need was supplied.

And it was never I, but He, who did it for me! There is no quick
recovery from a very great sorrow, but in each new day I was
permitted to see God's grace in something. Sometimes it was in
the smile of a friend or a little love token from my children or
maybe no more than a fragment of beautiful music. I learned
for myself the truth in that saying that we never lose those we
love. Our departed loved ones still help to color our world and
shape our thoughts by the impressions they have planted in our
memories.

When our sorrows are as bottomless as the sea, Christ is nearest and dearest. It is then that He speaks most clearly and holds
us closest. It is then that humble, grateful hearts overflow with
shouts of "Grace, grace!"

9
What God Hath Joined

This is now bone of my bones
And flesh of my flesh (Gen. 2:23).

The application of Christian principles is no place more needed today than in the time-honored, but often desecrated, institution of marriage. In our wash-and-wear world, often marriage vows are washed out as casually as last night's gravy stains; new relationships are donned with hardly a pause between. There has to be some explanation for this lack of commitment— the logical one being a lack of knowledge of why marriage exists in the first place. Failed marriages seem to happen most among people who have been perfectly content to live with false spiritual beliefs rather than undertake a serious search for God. The warning issued in 780 BC still applies: "My people are destroyed for lack of knowledge" (Hos. 4:6).

God's unconditional love teaches us that the deepest happiness in marriage comes from commitment, not from being "in love." The filled divorce courts give witness to the fact that many modern couples are putting the cart before the horse. Other couples, after years of marriage, have been able to say, "We thought we were in love then, but in no way could it compare to what we feel today." These couples undoubtedly made commitment their first priority, according to God's original plan. "Therefore shall a man leave his father and mother, and cleave unto his wife: and they shall be one flesh" (Gen. 2:24, KJV). The excitement of being in love multiplies itself endlessly when husband and wife grow in their commitment to one another.

Expectations influence our reactions to people and events. If I have planned a picnic for Saturday and I wake up to a thunderstorm, I am naturally not going to be thrilled. On the other hand, if I expected rain, I probably would have another plan ready to implement. The key here is flexibility. The inflexible picnicker will either run out and throw rocks at the clouds or take his disappointment out on people around him. A more flexible planner will cushion that first shock with the calm realism that plan B is ready to follow.

If you believe that marriage is no picnic, you are only half right by definition, for wedlock and picnics have a lot in common. Every picnic ought to have some idyllic time for peaceful loafing; but if that is all a picnic is for, why is it that no one ever goes on one without a basket of food? To have a good picnic requires fulfillment for the whole person: a setting that will please the aesthetic hunger of the eye, appetizing food for the body, and companionship for soul stimulus. That seems like the perfect situation, but it never is. When did you ever have a picnic without flies, ants, or an unexpected shower to cut short the fun?

Marriages are not really so different. People enter marriage with some common needs and expectations. But even in the best marriages, husbands and wives have to deal with unmet expectations which cause disappointment. Methods of coping with disappointment vary. How husbands and wives resolve their feelings of disappointment can strengthen or weaken their marriages.

If expectations for marriage are not the same, how can marriage be defined? Sometimes explaining what something is not is easier than explaining what it is, just as visualizing the absence of a desired object often clarifies its practical properties. Such is true when speaking of marriage. In a classroom of seniors where a graduate was planning marriage, an impulsive girl exclaimed, "Oh, I wish I could get married too! It sounds like fun!" The teacher, a confirmed bachelor lady of well-ripened years said, "Don't be silly. Marriage is not fun. It was never intended to be."

Even in my inexperience, I recognized the silliness of my classmate's remark, and I suspected the probability that marriage is not altogether fun. I also doubted the teacher's accuracy about what marriage was intended to be. I still do. Marriage ought to be more fun than anything, if what we mean by fun is a pleasurable state. It can be if we do not expect it to be just that all of the time. Nothing ever stays the same all the time. Not unless it is dead, and even then it is changing to another form of being. Only God changes not.

The everydayness of marriage is not usually expected by brides and grooms. They are so wrapped up in the warm, fuzzy whimsies they feel when they are together that they won't allow a doubt to enter their heads that this feeling will not continue forever.

They ignore the fact that the security they feel in each other's presence comes not only from themselves but also from previous relationships. The past has always done its work in molding our present state. Marrying is going to install a whole new security system, and no one knows yet if the locks are going to work.

Beal and Sally were confident that together they could work out all the surprises of the future. They were in love. They were realistic enough to know they would not always agree, but they had already weathered enough personality clashes to prove they could resolve their differences. Neither set of their parents had been divorced. They were willing to work for a comfortable home, children, enough prosperity to provide some luxuries, and, more admirably than many others, they were willing to wait until they could afford them. Their confidence was rightly placed in what they believed their own abilities to be. The fallacy of their perspective was one common to all of us. In looking at the projected goal, it is easy to forget the old unspoken law that just beyond the moss-covered log may lie a wily, sharp-mouthed serpent.

At the tender age of nine, I learned never to go walking on unproven ground without a measure of caution. I was trotting along my chosen route among the trees to my grandparent's home a mile away. The fallen log across the path was not too large to hop over easily; just an interesting diversion in my game of knighted horsemen charging the Bastile. On this particular cloudy morning, a light mist in the air exuded a clean, ferny smell, filling me with a sense of the magical, enchanted forest surrounding me. Remembering why I was going to Grandmother's house put sudden wings to my bare feet—the smells of the wet woods were no match for the anticipation of hot ginger cookies. I cleared the fallen log with one leap, surprising a stretched out rattlesnake.

My heart hammering, I stood transfixed a few yards away, listening to the hollow sounds of the snake's rattle. As frightened as I was, I felt amazement at the fluid speed with which he altered his position. Have you ever looked a coiled snake in the eye? At nine or ninety, the day you do, you will know the full meaning of danger.

To add to my childish terror, the mist turned into a light drizzle, just enough to drop spasmodically on the leaves, exciting my imagination. Every sound became another adversary creeping nearer. Rooted to the spot, afraid to move, I might still be there had not the rattlesnake become bored with the game. As he slithered away, I recovered my strength. The last half mile of that journey broke Olympic records, I feel certain. The experience also stamped the taste and smell of ginger cookies indelibly in my brain. After a bad confrontation is resolved, nothing comforts or commemorates as effectively as warm ginger cookies and cold buttermilk.

I tell this rattlesnake tale not so much to warn against dangerous snakes as to cultivate awareness of the potential danger in unexpected situations. The day two people marry, they picked up an enemy, the Enemy, the wily counterpart of my forest foe. It should come as no surprise that Satan hates the very essence of marriage—after all, marriage was God's idea. Just as I learned to carry a stick on my sylvan outings, it is wise to consider the best weapon against the sharp mouth of the Enemy. And trust me, the best weapon is not another sharp mouth.

I purposely left Beal and Sally back there to establish a home without interference, for of all the enemies of marriage, interference is one of the worst. Beal and Sally were careful about that. They saw enough of their parents to preserve the family ties, but they didn't involve their parents in decisions of their own domicile. The intrusion into their nest came from a most disarming source: friends or, in this case, Beal's friends. Why should marriage change the course of friendship? Everybody needs friends, and it was not as if his were unwilling to make concessions. Granted, Sally had rights; and if she expected old Beal to stay home at night, that could be arranged. Cards, pool, food, and drink could be just as much fun in a home. The added advantage home provided was that of not being locked out at closing time. If the party lasted longer than usual, the men would clean out the refrigerator and practice their culinary skills. Then if the hour were unusually late or the road home too far, everyone was adaptable to whatever was available. Not enough beds posed no problem; the sofa, a sleeping bag, or just a quilt was fine.

Was there ever a friend who could say that at no time he imposed or that he was never a little insensitive to the needs of others? These men, remember, were not uncaring poachers; they were genuine friends of long standing. Not envious of Beal's apparent happiness in an established home, they were just basking in the enjoyment of sharing it with him. Reaping the benefits, without having the responsibility of management. And Beal was holding on for dear life to that which he felt in some inexplicable way his marriage threatens. His friends became representative of his surrendered freedom and reassured him by their constant presence that he had actually given up nothing.

So where did this leave Sally? Obviously, if she were not sick of the sight of "the guys" by now, she soon would be. If she let her sour feelings show, Beal would be embarrassed and consider her to be selfish and spoiled. If she gave an ultimatum, a state of open warfare would erupt. Sally had a problem. It should have been a shared problem, which would have simplified it considerably, but since Beal could not see it as a problem, she had to handle it alone. What Sally had to do here was apply the Bible axiom of being "as wise as serpents and as harmless as doves" (Matt. 10:16).

At first, she could suggest gently that she was having difficulty stretching her food budget—maybe if they could just serve popcorn and Kool-Aid the next time someone dropped in— well, surely she would be able to figure something out. The worried look on her face didn't hurt a thing, and there was nothing fake about her concern; those wonderful well-meaning friends had turned her happy home into a community recreation hall.

This would not stop the flow of traffic through her house; all

Sally was doing was establishing a base from which to work. First the budget strain—and, suddenly, she was not getting enough sleep. She was too wise to complain; she just dozed off over dessert and let her hand rest gently in the pie. At bedtime, she was apologetically asleep before her head touched the pillow.

All this may seems a bit theatrical, but this is a real marriage-threatening situation which could be and often is addressed with harsh words and pouting, which cause hurt feelings all around. Any marriage that is not going to be a scrap to the finish has someone in it exercising a lot of diplomacy. In this instance, Sally let Beal be the hero who saw (with a little help) that marriage should change people—for the better. That was their purpose in getting married.

This is not necessarily a method to follow step by step. The important part of the solution is an attitude of compromise. Compromise is not a bad word or a bad attitude. What does marriage do but combine the qualities of two different beings in mutual agreement? All compromise does is combine concessions from both sides to adjust the problems.

10
Faults and Failures

Let all bitterness, wrath, anger, clamor, and evil speaking be put away from you, with all malice. And be kind to one another, tenderhearted, forgiving one another, just as God in Christ also forgave you (Eph. 4:31-32).

Nine years after the death of the first great love of my life, I met Al. In love from the first, we were soon married and propelled into a process of unlearning loneliness.

The next hardest thing to learning to live without those we love is learning to live with them. Those precious little habits that we hardly notice when there is space between us, suddenly cause a gnashing of teeth in close quarters. Till I became a wife, I never knew that leaving a cabinet door open or half closing a closet door could trigger justifiable homicide. I still don't always remember to close the doors, but I no longer see them as unimportant trifles.

You fall in the lucky three out of every twenty-five hundred if you can say with honesty that your spouse has not even one annoying habit. Don't identify yourselves, because The Enemy will immediately assign someone to your case.

Habits are good or bad, depending upon who is evaluating them. Mine never really seem very significant to me; consequently, I am surprised when they become an issue to someone else. I can see how snoring could disrupt sleep. I can see how gossiping could hurt people terribly. I can easily understand the destructiveness of lying and the agony caused by drinking. None of these are my frailties to any recognizable degree, so I find it amazing that a little thing like visiting on the telephone or offering alternative plans could upset anyone.

The most trouble I have ever stirred up began in a refreshment stop on a bus tour out of Puerta Vallerta, Mexico. Before the bus stopped, thirsty travelers were set up by the driver's glowing description of the delicious, marvelous drink to be purchased there: "In this life, you have never tasted anything like it!" (That part was true.)

By the time Al and I got off the bus, people had queued up in two directions. We drifted into the nearest line, which turned out to be the longest. That should have told me something. But in my usual inimitable misconstruction, I suggested, "Let's get in that short line; we will get to the drink stand sooner."

When I make these alternative proposals, it never occurs to me that the habit and not the idea itself upsets Al. In my mind, all I am doing is looking for the best possibility. To him, I am sure it seems that I want to be boss and make final decisions. I am trying to train myself to see this through Al's eyes. It must be frustrating to have the simplest decisions suddenly complicated by a new set of possibilities to consider.

As might be expected, I had talked us into the wrong queue; the short line was for the rest rooms. By the time we discovered that, the drink line was much longer, which was more bad news for me because next to having the game plan changed, Al's prime annoyance is waiting in line. True to the bus driver's prediction, I had never tasted anything like that drink. This clearly was not one of my better days! With a pleading look, I silently passed the pineapple hull full of liquid fire to a hulk of a man who looked tough enough to handle it and climbed back on the bus. I made no further suggestions.

The reason it is so hard for us to learn to live with others is because it takes self-discipline to accept them as they are. When what they are annoys us, we don't want to adjust our attitudes; we want to change them. Perhaps God made us all different to teach us acceptance of others. Clearly we are not all the way we ought to be, maybe none of us, but not one of us will change anything until we ourselves see the need for change. And even then, we cannot expect instant success because the Enemy is well aware of what is happening. For years he has conned me into withdrawing with bruised feelings after my good ideas are rejected, which made more trouble for me. That just encouraged me to come up with better ideas. What I needed was to take a long look at why what I was doing was not working. It doesn't matter what your intentions are if your method is failing. In anybody's ball park, the numbers on the scoreboard tell the story. If my wonderful suggestions are resented, then Al's way of doing things must be best for me simply because I like it when he is happy with me. And he is always happy with me when I agree with him.

Being agreeable is an art. Not necessarily agreeing with everything, but being agreeable. With practice, even a child can learn to disagree agreeably; it's that simple.

I learned how valuable this can be from the experience of a friend. Dena was thoroughly convinced that to be an obedient Christian meant to tithe her income. Not employed herself, she tried to convince her husband that the Lord needed a tenth of what they earned to continue His work. Bob owned a small restaurant. He believed in the work of the church, but felt that the financial bind he stayed in prevented the luxury of giving away 10 percent of what he felt he needed more. Dena wisely accepted the authority of his decision. At the same time she gently expressed her opinion, with the hope that it could be worked out later.

A few weeks later, a discussion on tithing came up in her church study group. One member whose husband did not tithe said, "He just does not know he tithes. I get it together one way or another, out of grocery money, his pocket, or tack it on to household expenses." Dena repeated this to Bob that night, along with her opinion that her friend was wrong to take the money that way. "I find it hard to believe that God wants us to steal in order to give to Him."

Bob thought for a minute, then asked, "If we are fair, isn't the money really as much hers as his?"

The following Sunday, without a word, Bob checked the week's receipts, opened the cash register, and took out 10 percent of his profit for their church. Bob and Dena may have had 10 percent less money for themselves, but the bills got paid, and everything seemed to go on as usual, except that their household was just about the happiest you would find anywhere.

> "And prove Me now in this,"
> Says the Lord of hosts,
> "If I will not open for you the
>   windows of heaven
> And pour out for you such blessing
> That there will not be room enough
>   to receive it" (Mal. 3:10).

My point is, Dena got what she really wanted: to do what she believed to be right. When we are sure we are doing what is right, the rest comes easier, just a natural result of practicing the art of being agreeable.

I saw Dena not long ago and was glad to hear that she learned, about the same time I did, that God really does not need that tenth of what we make. He just wants us to have the blessing of acknowledging where it all comes from. He can hold out just fine if we dig a hole and bury everything we get our hands on. He made that clear when He said:

> If I were hungry, I would not tell you;
> For the world is Mine, and all its fullness (Ps. 50:12).

Some women, once the marriage vows are spoken, develop a compulsion to change everything. Many men only want to remain the way they were. Women might think about that in their consideration of lifetime mates. If men come straight from their adoring mothers who looked on serving their needs as a holy calling, that is the interpretation the grooms will put on, "I take thee, Tom. . . ."

That is why I wish, instead of indulging their every whim, mothers, and also fathers, would put the little guys in training toward becoming good husbands. Of course, this wishful thinking is unrealistic unless those same mothers and fathers are teaching their daughters to become good wives.

The women's movement of recent years has brought some changes that benefit society, but it has far less impact inside the home than is generally supposed. Feelings cannot be legislated. Socially, a man may be pressured into operating under established rules; but in the privacy of his home, he will use only the dictates of his own conscience as a guideline.

I accept the biblical concept of the male authority figure within the home. No, at first I accepted it. Over the years, my attitude has changed; I now endorse and embrace it because in my experience it has worked as no other system could. Why would I want the final word? If we could check statistics on all the crucial decisions indiscriminately made by people, shock at the number of wrong ones would probably scare out of us all incentive to ever make another one. When decisions are to be made at our house, my influence is always a factor, but I do not want the burden of judgment to be mine alone. Credit for right choices is nice—blame for the bad ones not so good. I am more comfortable sharing both.

Women who have trouble accepting the man as head of the family have usually received their training from a woman troubled by the same attitude. Of course, no woman should allow herself to become a doormat, but of those who do, many had visible warning signals that they ignored. An overbearing, egotistical bully does not rise up full-blown from the honeymoon bed. In even a short acquaintance, there must have been some character trait that was overlooked before the ceremony.

I am not making a conscious effort to confuse the issue of who the head of the family should be, but, rather, attempting to state that totalitarianism by either sex cannot fulfill the purpose of marriage. The attempt to totally control will result in a power struggle whether or not it is visible to the eye.

My own father was driven for years, no doubt, by a false concept of the moral law of marriage conduct; for all that time, he was convinced that he reigned supreme, though it brought him little satisfaction. Had he been able to look at it objectively, he could have known that he was being resisted, however passively. My mother was expert in passive resistance. Seeming to conform, there was always in her bearing a dignity of spirit that belied any air of servitude. Only after Dad got straightened out in his mind that the Architect of marriage is the true authority were they able to achieve a mutually conciliatory relationship. Two more unified elderly people could not be found. I am grateful for the happiness they found in the twilight of their lives.

So there could be no misunderstanding, the Bible clearly compares the role of the wife to that of the church in its relation to Christ. "For the husband is head of the wife, as also Christ

is head of the church; and He is the Savior of the body. Therefore, just as the church is subject to Christ, so let the wives be
to their own husbands in everything. Husbands, love your wives
as Christ also loved the church and gave Himself for it" (Eph.
5:23-25). A lot more is said in Ephesians about loving and nour-
ishing and cherishing; and none of it is wasted on me. For those
misguided souls who fight for the right to be boss half the time
or half-boss all the time, I have but this to say: just give me a
man who will take the position with me that Christ takes with
the church and you can have all your so-called equality!

I believe that everything God began has the formula for success built into it when His plan is followed. To reverse that order
will as naturally invite disaster. It does no good to argue that it
might be better another way; hypothetical situations are not
reality. Whether you agree with the way God set something has
no bearing. God said wives should be submissive to their husbands and husbands are to love their wives as Christ loves the
church. I believe this is essential in reaching a rich and beautiful
companionship because I trust God's authority.

> Every wise woman builds her house,
> But the foolish pulls it down
> with her hands (Prov. 14:1).

From my viewpoint, I am always puzzled when a seemingly
intelligent woman, will with apparent deliberation, tear her
house down around her. I have seen educated, attractive, socially acceptable women with a biological need for marriage
become destructive toward what they appear to want most.
Cassie was one of those.

Cassie pounced on marriage with all the enthusiasm of a cat
with a cornered mouse, leaving no doubt that it was hers for
keeps, to extract from it all life's mortal joys. If you have ever
watched a cat with a mouse, your sympathies are instinctively

with the mouse, if only because you know he is overmatched. The cat teases, acting playful and indifferent by turns, but always ready to smack the mouse back into his corner if he shows an interest in anything outside their immediate circle. We know what is going to eventually happen. The mouse is going to be swallowed if he does not find some avenue of escape. His chances of escape will increase when he realizes the cat's intentions.

What Brian should have realized before marrying Cassie is that along with cats and mice, people are also obliged to act out of their natures. For a realistic picture of Cassie, Brian needed to look at these three things: how she reacted to those who crossed her, how she responded when adverse conditions arose, and how she related to her Creator. When these characteristics are brought into line, the real person, the person who will motivate all the action, can be seen. Brian was not unaware of this. Without admitting Cassie's personality flaws verbally, he still instinctively knew they existed. He liked the way he felt when he pleased her, enough to convince himself that he could handle the temper tantrums when he didn't. *Cassie just needs time to grow up,* he had told himself, *and I have plenty of time to wait for that; meanwhile we could be enjoying a happy relationship together, right?* Wrong.

First off, he needed to see that Cassie, not really being related to her Creator, had no intention of making any effort to grow up in the spiritual sense. Marriage is a spiritual state as well as a physical state, and it can only be ideally lived out by Spirit-led people. When we see those who appear to be making a good marriage who do not have a personal relationship with God, we need to consider this. I could put on a Kansas City Royal's uniform and sit on the bench in the dugout next to George Brett and look as if I belonged on the team. It would work until I had to take my time at bat or at third base. Then I would be in a situation beyond my capabilities.

We can understand that if we are hauled into court we are going to need a lawyer. If we are inexperienced at mechanics and buy something that must be assembled, we had better read the instructions. We must recognize that a spiritual institution cannot work successfully when purely physical rules are applied to it.

Cassie was selfish, head-strong and childish—and these are only her better qualities. Brian had a speaking acquaintance with the Lord but had not learned to listen well. That is the reason he missed "Do not be unequally yoked together with unbelievers" (2 Cor. 6:14) in the instructions to Christians. He stuck his head in the sand, ostrich fashion, not having noticed what a perfect target this makes of the ostrich's hindermost. After a dozen years of being knocked down more times than he could bear to think about, Brian succumbed to the pressure; he gave up.

His dream of reaching a satisfying plateau of communication had died so gradually that in the end, Brian was hardly aware of its passing. Only a dull, aching void remained as a reminder that life's deepest expression was lost without having been fully found.

Pain can sometimes be cathartic, giving us the will to save ourselves. If a mouse had the deductive power to take a long-range view, he may, after enduring the cat's tortures for a time, consider standing on his hind legs and fighting back. Rage and frustration would bolster his puniness, at least enough to challenge the cat's brutish nature. An intelligent mouse would see that his demise is imminent in any event. A very intelligent mouse would see the futility of sacrificing himself on such a meaningless altar and use every ounce of strength he had left, to escape. That is what Brian did.

Poor Cassie! After all the years of contrived discontent, she had to deal with the real thing, with good reason, and all alone, having effectively pulled her house down around her.

Avoidable calamities are no different from the legitimate ones in physical damage, but they are different in their emotional impact. I can better live with misfortune that came to me uninvited and over which I had no control. To accept personal responsibility for lost opportunities and failed joys is shattering to my peace of mind.

Because Cassie taught school, I was shocked that she let this happen. I have so much admiration for formal education that I am always forgetting that some of the people who instruct our children how to live would not qualify for an eighth grade diploma in actual practice. Cassie's letters of learning in history and languages were not based on a practiced experience of either. Having lost touch with her in recent years, I wonder if she ever learned to use proficiently the required universal language, the language of love. "Though I speak with the tongues of men and of angels, and have not love, I have become as sounding brass or a clanging cymbal" (1 Cor. 13:1).

There are many Cassies and not all are females. I believe there is hope for them. That is not misguided confidence in their ability to change themselves, but belief in what a loving Heavenly Father can do for them if they will place themselves in his hands.

Then it happened one evening that David arose from his bed and walked on the roof of the king's house. And from the roof he saw a woman bathing, and the woman was very beautiful to behold. (2 Sam. 11:2).

A great many men seem to have a concept of beauty that is limited to the bloom of youth. Married men as well as single

men often seem to have this concept. This false idea of spring-
time as the panacea for all ills, and especially for their own
advancing age's negative side effects, is the Enemy's most sub-
tle and most lethal weapon. While women do not seem as vul-
nerable to this dangerous attraction of youth as men, women
are also suseptible.

There is no use appealing to a sense of fairness on this subject.
Once a person's head is turned by flattering words and implied
promises, reinforced by a proportionate mix of innocence and
experience, he or she is in no condition to assess fairness. At that
stage, equity has become an expendable issue. Because the Enemy's recruits have made inroads on the alter ego of men or
women, we cannot expect such people to remember that God's
computers are perfectly oiled and running steadily. Much,
much later, one will be reminded that "whatever a man sows,
that he will also reap" (Gal. 6:7). There will be plenty of time
to reflect on all of that when spring has come and gone, and the
rigors of winter have set in.

All that time for reflection can be credited to the efficiency
of the Enemy. In some instances he does his work so well that
unfortunate consequences follow.

(1) Children, if there are any, become bitter. They are no
longer able to exhibit pride in someone who has embarrassed
and disillusioned them. In instances where they were pushed
aside by the expediencies of the current romance, they may be
permanently alienated. In some cases, they lose touch with
their own sense of worth, questioning the values they were
taught to honor, which is the most tragic result of all. Fairness
is here most abused. Someone will pay; if first it is the children,
remember those well-oiled computers. They are still running.
The Master Programmer will justly determine accountability.

(2) Business may suffer, due to overall neglect or lack of attention to details. People who have worked hard all their lives for

financial security have been known, at the drop of an eyelash, to toss away all they have gained.

(3) Finally, in the time of life that was designed to be the richest part, the errant one discovers the saddest truth of all—he or she may not really fit in any place. The friends one started out with may be uncomfortable in attempts to share a new life, fearful of calling the new love by the old name, or of reminiscing aloud about good times gone by.

Roving husbands and wives, heaven forbid that both should be under one roof, though that would seem the more fair distribution, have in common the attitude that they are where they are through no fault of their own; fate arranged it. It will not be easy to convince these people that things do not just happen, though it appears that way to some degree in some instances. Sometimes a comforting shoulder takes on more significance than intended and turns into a psychological need. When this happens, the response is from feelings and emotions, which will always clamor for attention more loudly than the spiritual presence. We do not like admitting it, but such situations could not carry us away without some help from ourselves. Scattered and isolated incidents of infidelity do not just come together like the dry bones of Ezekiel's vision, unless we will it so.

To destroy the trust of a husband's or wife's faithfulness is to destroy a vital part of the person. The very sensitive person will often close his or her eyes and ears to what is obvious double-dealing, believing this to be the first line of defense. Dealt a bad hand, he or she often chooses to play it out, for the stakes are high.

Break an egg even a tiny crack and you increase its vulnerability. Breaking marriage vows has the same effect on a marriage. The hard-boiled can tolerate more abuse in the egg basket or the marriage. It is incredible that anyone who has a warm, sensitive, satisfying relationship with another would risk it for any reason.

The Enemy agrees completely. That is why all his agents are incredibly attractive and persuasive.

11
Fruit from the Spice Garden

"Awake, O north wind,
And come O south!
Blow upon my garden,
That its spices may flow out.
Let my beloved come to his garden
And eat its pleasant fruits"
(Song of Sol 4:16).

I grew up in a family where reading was encouraged simply by the absence of other forms of entertainment. I read everything, Tarzan, mysteries, romance, adventure, poetry, the Bible. I list the Bible last because I read it least. I know I am a lot smarter now than I was then because I have reversed the order of the list.

In those romantic stories for which my appetite grew in my teens, the heroine was often serenaded by a nightingale. I don't think I have ever heard a nightingale, but I used to imagine that a mockingbird sounded like one in the dead of night. The story went that the nightingale always sang his sweetest when the night was darkest. A mockingbird's song in the middle of the night was different from his day songs. Such sheer melodic Orphean tones had to be the mockingbird's imitation of the nightingale. (Orpheus was a Greek who could charm the bark off of trees.)

There was a reason for the nightingale's euphonic midnight sweetness. In utter darkness, song is most needed. When no known way is visible to us, a melody in the heart will uplift us. The Bible can do the same thing for us; it is our nightingale.

Marriage is the only pursuit of life in which truth must be camouflaged as compassion. The idea of honesty having to pose as anything else may sound dishonest, but whoever said that truth hurts was right; it often does. Lovers are so sensitive to each other that blunt honesty can wound, irreparably. For those times of bruised feelings or open anger, a nightingale would be a definite convenience to have around. Since there usually isn't one outside the window just waiting for a lover's quarrel, it is good to have one in your heart—those words of counsel from God that give a song.

We always say "tell me the truth," when what we mean is "love me enough to overlook what I really am." And often, lovers do just that, but it is not the best way to handle problems. In fact, that is only encouraging Cassieism—remember Cassie? Faults, like illnesses, should never be given a chance to grow. When faults are harmful to character, they can be as destructive to a happy marriage as a critical illness is to the body.

To ignore the truth is to defer trouble till a later date, but not much later, because the Enemy is not noted for patience. When he sees a little problem, he has all kinds of insidious maneuvers to start building it into a big one.

Perhaps the single most important contributing factor to a secure marriage is communication. Communication is the heart of marriage. From the first verbal "I love you" to the sexual merging, it is the coming together of separate souls to become one, communicating to each other that they belong together. This shared oneness will accomplish three very good things if it is based on truth: (1) Greater pleasure in each other. (2) Ease in resolving conflicting views. (3) More understanding of each other's feelings.

Only honest feelings can produce the best kind of relationship. When conflict exerts pressure, real feelings begin to emerge. When you squeeze an orange, you get orange juice. In the final analysis, that is what you want and expect from a relationship—consistent honesty. If a relationship is to remain strong under pressure, it has to be consistently honest.

Sometimes we must make facts known that will not be pleasant or flattering to hear. When a hurting truth is spoken, it must be done with love if it is of any value at all; to use the truth spitefully destroys its benefit because it is being subversely manipulated to cause pain. Ephesians 4:15 tells us how to do it: "But, speaking the truth in love, [we] may grow up in all things into Him who is the head—Christ." If our real purpose is to hurt, we can get a fight started with just a word. If we speak the truth in love, even if it is at first refused, our ability to communicate remains undamaged. When we love one another, the motivation for correcting faults takes on a benevolence of character. We are distressed at wrongdoing in those we love because of the harm it does them and not just because it annoys us.

When we have the habit of "speaking the truth in love," even if our tentmate is momentarily upset, we are going to find within ourselves a healing quality that reaches out to pull us together again. The Old Testament speaks of "balm in Gilead" as a medicine for the sick and hurting ones. That balm is a spirit of love within that looks past one's own hurt to the feelings of others, even when they have brought their miseries on themselves. Showing this kind of love may not result in instant healing every time, especially if the relationship is deeply torn, for some wounds require a ton of balm. And all the patience a person possesses.

It never pays be angered by another person's anger. When one person in a love relationship temporarily loses his ability to control his emotions, he needs compassion, not correction. We all know that the best help is that which helps us to help ourselves. This is one of the strongest reinforcements to marriage. The Enemy tries to convince us that fighting fire with fire works better than soothing "balm." We are not dealing with forest fires, but private confrontations between separate members of one flesh.

I wonder if Simon Peter had a few marital problems of his own, he gave such sensible advice in 1 Peter 3. He practically promised that even if some should absolutely refuse to be harmonious at first, they can be won over by gentleness and love. Becoming conversant with Peter's personality gives us some license to surmise that it took a lot of supportive patience to mold Peter into the saint he became. We clearly see Jesus' patience with Peter, but Jesus' Spirit in others may also be seen. Isn't it possible that Mrs. Peter was one of those spiritual persons of whom it was said, "Brethren, if a man is overtaken in any trespass, you who are spiritual restore such a one in a spirit of gentleness, considering yourself lest you also be tempted" (Gal. 6:1)?

To always love is much easier than to always show love. If we love, we love; it is the state of our nature. But showing love often depends on the state of our fickle emotions. We become angry, jealous, or sometimes just plain mean and flare up, blotting out any sight of love. If we are ever going to light candles, we ought to do it for the darkness. Not that a candle does any harm to the sunlight but because a candle's purpose is best served in the dark. So, what is love's purpose?

If you are truly in love and find yourself too often miserable because of it, there is something wrong. Analyze for yourself what love is. Is it getting or giving? We know "God is love" (1

John 4:8), so one look at Him will answer the question decisively. Love involves several emotions in one, all basically good. When love is allowed to stray into anger, jealousy, and selfishness, all bad emotions, it perverts itself, becoming the Enemy's tool. In his hands, it will tear and hurt until it leaves you weakened and helpless. When you turn it over to the Enemy, what else can you expect? He is a destroyer.

True love has the patience to work its way through painful experiences while remaining kind. When we are hurt, our first impulse is to inflict a few bruises of our own. This only works well in war. Love and war have nothing but intensity in common. If I am quick to drag love to the battleground, it tells me something about myself that I do not like. If I remain kind, not much fighting will get done. Fighting in a kindly way is next to impossible.

"Love does not envy" (1 Cor. 13:4). If the thought of envying one you love makes no sense to you, you are catching the spirit of the meaning of the great scriptural essay on love. Envy is the resentment we feel for someone who has something we lack. Usually, a morally responsible person will guard against sulking over good fortunes of others, but how analytically do we examine the quick anger we feel over their superior way of looking at things? When we are in conflict with others, we want iron to sharpen iron. We feel censured when our grumpiness is countered with gentleness. Our pride scorns such tenderness, compelling us toward disrupting the proffered peace. Pride always produces the sword, never the plowshare. The desire to dominate, rooted in pride, will first destroy peace within, then turn its feuding outward. Peace is the gift of God to the humble. "God resists the proud, But gives grace to the humble" (Jas. 4:6). As surely as envy is its own punishment, love is its own reward. When we see the grace of character that answers sharpness with gentleness, we know it was hard bought and paid for in installments of practice, practice, practice.

Courtroom drama may be exciting to watch on television, but it is deadly when acted out in the home. When husbands and wives create a detective-agency atmosphere with suspicious natures, they can expect love to shrivel up. Marriage can survive hunger, sickness, fire, flood, and any number of painful calamities, but it cannot tolerate for long a mean, suspicious lack of trust. Love "thinks no evil" (1 Cor. 13:5), and if you will think about it, the times you are comfortable and happy are those times when you are with those who believe in you. In this atmosphere, we are at our best.

Marriage is the basket in which love is carried. From it we take out the choicest fruit to offer our beloved. To understand the true value of a marriage, one must stand alone, stripped of all supportive companionship. Only then can a true comparison be made between having and having not. It never does us harm to retreat in our minds to the what-once-was place. Nothing makes us so aware of our present blessings as remembering the absence of them.

When two people are trying to find more closeness with each other, the best way is for each to cultivate a consciousness of Christ as Teacher. The key to happy marriage is logically found in the Scriptures, for the Bible is a handbook on marriage. It tunes people in on the same wave length, bringing them to a unity of mind, body, and spirit. These components make up our natures and when any part becomes healthier, the whole nature is made stronger. A right spirit in both partners will bond their relationship without conspicuous discord because they are of the same mind.

How do you think one hundred trained musicians who have never seen each other can come together, and without one practice, play Handel's *Messiah* to perfection? If they are all playing in perfect tune with the score, the harmony is there, not because they follow each other, but because they are attentive to the right standard. For two people to reach oneness, this same kind of focus is necessary.

To set oneness as a goal almost always assures success because, once experienced, each partner will be much too challenged by its possibilities to ever carelessly run the risk of losing it. Can you imagine someone being told that a million dollars waits at the post office for him, but his refusing to pick up the mail? We are much more foolish to neglect the simple requirements of reaching a beautiful relationship.

The necessity for Jesus Christ is absolute in every life that is seeking fulfillment. Only the degree of commitment is in question. How far He will go with you in your search is limited only by your own design. How far are you willing for Him to go?

The idea of entering marriage without Christ is equal to my wading into the capricious waters of the Missouri River unable to swim; the first swirling eddy would swallow me. Marriage on a performance level can be compared to any other institution in this respect: Its success will depend upon who is in charge. If Christ is at its center, it cannot fail. "Search from the book of the Lord, and read:/Not one of these shall fail" (Isa. 34:16). When people think they are too smart to go by the old rules, they show their ignorance. Today's standard of intelligence usually includes only linguistic and logical-mathematical skills, but we stand on the threshold of advances that can change the entire spectrum of life on this planet. These are areas of intelligence that people will accept because they can see the results of their use to improve the quality of life. As important as these are, spiritual intelligence takes priority over them; but people generally refuse to acknowledge its practicability.

All forms of intelligence have their place, all are needed, but

without spiritual understanding, not one is capable of giving
you the abundant life.

> There's a time to listen
> And a time to share . . .
> A time to reach out
> To show that you care.
> A time to work—
> And a time to play,
> Time for reflection,
> And time to pray.
> Take time to be intimate;
> To know and be known . . .
> For love won't survive
> If it isn't shown.
> Love's union is built
> By sharing its worth,
> These times all together
> Make a heaven on earth.

A discussion of the heaven on earth we want, without addressing the important role of sex in it, would project an incomplete picture.

Husbands and wives both suffer when too much emphasis is placed on any one facet of the relationship at the expense of all the others. An ideal union must include satisfying sexual activity but to use it as a bludgeon or a tool cheapens its value. Everybody has expectations of what this area of life should be, but the reality is often disappointing, continuing throughout the marriage, because many people assume that problems of sex will resolve themselves with time.

The key to perfect sexual union with one's mate is as surely found in 1 Corinthians 13 as is the guide to our dealings with all others. The more intimate the relationship, the more important our spiritual perception becomes. Not motivated by kindness, but always characterized by it, sex finds its most satisfying response in those who seek to please each other more than self.

This involves complete concentration. I honestly believe that when this desire to please takes precedence over self-gratification, the rewards of delight and lasting pleasure in each other will surpass our power to describe. Our joy in giving always travels full circle to the joy of receiving. Wanting to please, by either husband or wife, is never a passive emotion but a lively awareness.

I am not concerned about the mechanics of lovemaking. Regardless of all the instructions the books about sex can give, prepared hearts are the only prerequisite to sexual fulfillment. Look at love as a gift. As God gave love to you, holding back nothing, you give to your beloved.

My first marriage was to a wonderful jack-of-all-trades who knew enough about a lot of things to try several occupations: restaurant management, railroad brakeman, diesel engineer, carpenter, farmer, cement worker, law officer, and finally returning to the restaurant business before dying of a massive coronary occlusion at the age of forty. Of all the things he knew something about, what he knew best was how to keep life exciting and worthwhile for his wife and children. For eighteen years, I thought this man knew everything! In the years since, I have realized that it just seemed that way because he took whatever he had and did the best he could with it.

After his death, people streamed past his bier for a last farewell. They were there not because he was a great business success but because he had touched each one in some helpful way. Several months later, I remarked to our pastor friend, "I placed too much emphasis on his importance. I guess it angered God." The young man wisely protested, "It was not that way at all. God always knew when his time on earth would end, so he purposely sent him to someone to share that time with who would make him feel ten feet tall. And aren't you glad you did?"

I am especially glad my friend was so wise because that little remark has been like a key to doors tightly locked against love and friendship. Do you know that many people are "difficult" because they are afraid to love? Somewhere in the past, they have given themselves and lost and feel betrayed by love. Love never betrays; people do.

The key of loving enough to make your partner feel good about himself or herself will go a long way toward opening up a beautiful relationship in which sex is an undercurrent of joy, always present, always surfacing at just the right time.

Do you really appreciate your partner? Something attracted you once. When husbands and wives lose their desire for each other physically, it is not the end unless one or both want it to be. It is always tragic when one of them closes the door to restoring the romance, especially if the dissatisfied one will not take a completely honest look at the reason for it. I wonder how many unhappy marriage partners would believe how much they contribute to their own boredom at home. I don't swallow the theory that either has the right to look for excitement elsewhere when home is not "life at the Ritz" every day. When married couples have to go elsewhere to find entertainment, they need to recognize that they are headed for trouble. Once the party pattern is established, the old ego has already swelled too much to enjoy simpler pleasures. Even dull married people ought to be smart enough to create their own excitement. Consider it a challenge to create fun for your family!

It is a miracle that Al and I survived our first two years together. Looking back, I think we had only one thing in common: we wanted to marry each other. I had been a widow for nine years; he was recently divorced. My former marriage of eighteen years was steady, secure, without a break; his, a history of numerous separations.

In every argument, I was given the distinct impression that my position, at best, was only temporary. The message I was sending was that he had decided to marry me and he couldn't get out of the marriage without me and I was not quitting. Can you imagine such a stalemate? If the wonderful times of deeply satisfying oneness had not been occurring with regularity throughout the whole thing, we might have given up. I cannot think of a worse tragedy. We are approaching nineteen years together, of which at least three-fourths have been filled with a genuine brightness and wonder to make us glad every day to be alive at this time, in this place, and in our situation.

We had found, disappointingly at first, that separately we were not perfect people. As time passed, we have learned that together, in harmony, we come as near our ideal of a perfect relationship as any two people could wish.

12
But God . . .

But God, who is rich in mercy, because of His great love with which He loved us, even when we were dead in trespasses, made us alive together with Christ (by grace you have been saved) (Eph. 2:4-5).

I am not well versed in Greek mythology, preferring truth to even the present-day baseball and apple pie variety of myths. But I am intrigued by the fact that the most elaborate fantasy makers feel a need to explain God.

Orpheus was a charmer in ancient Greece, who played the lyre so sweetly that animals and even rocks and trees followed him. In theory, the Greek mystery religion, Orphism, made the important point that man is both good and evil. In this religious persuasion, immortality was achieved by pure moral living, combined with ritualism. The most advocated cult ritual involved eating raw flesh to achieve union with God.

None of us can advance far into the day without seeing the good and evil warring for supremacy within our own natures. "We all once conducted ourselves in the lusts of our flesh, fulfilling the desires of the flesh and of the mind, and were by nature children of wrath, just as the others" (Eph. 2:3). I think that describes us all at some point in our lives. Small wonder that we see so many who claim to know Christ, but have so little of His joy in their lives. More misery could not be accumulated than the natural by-product of all the collective inordinate desires of these nominal Christians. How little hope there would be for any one of us without the next two words in verse 4, "But God. . . ." The writer then explained our status in Christ.

In our former state, we "walked according to the course of this world, according to the prince of the power of the air, the spirit who now works in the sons of disobedience." That "prince" is the Enemy, whose sovereign power is limited to the lower regions of our lives, "the course of this world" (v. 2).

But God raised us above the serfdom of sin "and made us sit together in the heavenly places in Christ Jesus" (v. 6). This is the victory that every Christian can claim; it is bought by Jesus and paid for with His blood. "For whatever is born of God overcomes the world. And this is the victory that has overcome the world—our faith" (1 John 5:4).

It is ironic that our nature insists on taking credit for the good that comes out of every activity in which we are involved. Reading the Psalms has a humbling effect. For a lesson in true humility, try reading Psalm 119:97-104. The psalmist recognized that he was wiser than his enemies, but he saw that the wisdom came from God's law. The psalmist knew that his understanding was greater than all his teachers, but only because he meditated on God's Word.

It is never a reflection on teachers, but an honor to them when a pupil can pass them in learning. My calling from God is to attempt to teach the Scriptures, but I know that in the arena of spiritual knowledge, the only lesson others learn from me will be in what they see that Christ has done for me.

Even as we read that our faith has overcome the world, the source of our faith comes to mind. "So then faith comes by hearing, and hearing by the word of God" (Rom. 10:17). We cannot, in all honesty, even take credit for our faith.

There is much good to be enjoyed in the world, but the spirit of sensuality is that part of the world that must be overcome. It is that world that is an obstacle between us and God, and to just sit down and try to wish it away only makes us miserable. Joshua learned a lesson for all of us when the Lord answered his crying and complaining with: "Get up. Why do you lie thus on your face?" (Josh 7:10). Self-pity is not only demeaning to us but also is displeasing to God.

To say that we have overcome means that a new plateau of experience has been reached. In some situations a triumph may be lasting, but in the spiritual realm, we can never say conclusively that we have won. What we can reach for is mastery over our natures on a day-to-day basis. This is not a monitoring system that is constantly checking the state of our morality, but rather, a never-ceasing awareness of the presence of Christ.

We see the significance of this when we compare it with a consciousness of those we love most. While our children are in school, we are not with them; they are physically out of sight, but not for one moment are they completely forgotten. The knowledge that they are depending on us motivates our action and generates our feelings. When they are released from our conscious minds, they are still lodged in the subconscious.

In this same manner, the person of the Holy Spirit is communicating His guidance in a powerful way to our brains if our wills are so committed. The highest function of the mind is its reasoning power. A Christ-directed subconscious, connected to what we know intellectually, gives us the complete message that we need instantaneously.

Such an electrifying possibility can turn defeated living into victorious living. The difference in the Joshua lying on his face and the Joshua who took the whole land of Canaan was his trust in the promise we, too, can claim: "I will not [fail] you or forsake you" (Josh. 1:5).

We have all seen those who seem charged with power and who seem to have a magic touch. They were not chosen at random to receive greater blessings than ordinary people. If you could observe the creative processes at work in their minds, you would find that they have positive, deep-seated convictions that they have goals worth fighting for.

This is the very point of failure with so many. Instead of concentrating on the goal, they allow their attention to be drawn to their own capabilities. Our subconscious externalizes those thoughts which are the most strongly implanted in it. This is why repetition of God's Word is so valuable to us; we need it so ingrained that its power can be transmitted to our conscious thoughts. The technique of repetition is needed in developing Christ consciousness, for thoughts are often as elusive as quicksilver and easily forgotten. I want help in my everyday life, not just visionary thoughts to comfort me at rest. What I need is power, and sometimes I need it quickly.

Studying different translations of the Bible can aid our understanding. The King James Version translates Romans 12:12c as "continuing instant in prayer." I like that translation because it implies instant help in answer to prayers.

Al has worked in the construction industry most of his life. Consequently, he has seen many close calls in this dangerous occupation and has had a few himself. The ones he takes the most pleasure in telling involve miraculous rescues, the kind of experiences that cause people to shake their heads and murmur, "Unexplainable." Al can explain them.

On one occasion, Al was in the fifteen foot deep bin beneath a rock crusher, attempting to dislodge the stone that had frozen together in the sub-zero weather. He had closed the bottom of the bin so the crushed road rock would not pour out while he pried it loose.

Al was standing atop the rock, pecking away at it with a

crowbar, when the rock broke loose suddenly. He plunged downward, rock falling in around him. Low in the bin in an upright position with one arm holding the crowbar overhead, Al's other arm was pinned at his side. Rock kept caving in on him. To add to his terror, it was getting dark, and all the workers had gone but his brother and one other man. Even before he cried for help, his instantaneous thought was, *Lord Jesus, help me.*

The crushed rock then completely covered Al, except for his upper face. He was barely able to breathe, the tremendous weight of cold stone burying him. Wouldn't you say "instant in prayer" most nearly expressed his petition? It is one of Al's favorite verses.

The rescue was frantic and suspenseful. The two men at first tried pulling Al out, but that was impossible. While one held on to him from above, the other opened the bin below, allowing enough rock to spill out, releasing him. This is not a story he enjoys remembering, except that God was there.

Great deliverances have a way of expanding grateful hearts, building up a desire to share with others this mighty force for good. One of the hardest things a believer has to accept is that sometimes those we love most in the world will have no part of what we know to be the truth. This does not leave us without recourse. A simple analysis will immediately suggest to us a course of positive action.

If there is someone whom we know to be lost, we first need to establish in our own minds just how concerned we are and what our position of influence is. I always hesitate to use the word *lost*, but Jesus used it to describe unbelievers on several occasions, stating as His purpose, "The Son of Man has come to save that which was lost" (Matt. 18:11).

If our concern is deep, and if we already have an established rapport, the next step must be suggested by the Father Himself.

Too many times we go off on our own without any clear direction from Him and then wonder why we fail. I think most of our failures happen because we have been taught or somehow have conditioned ourselves to see anything less than immediate success as unacceptable. And why not? This is the most important endeavor of our lives. What we must remember is that we are not always allowed to see the results of our labors.

When we lift up in prayer the ones about whom we are concerned, we have taken the initiative in making ourselves available. We need never be afraid of being offensive when we offer ourselves as servants, instead of aggressively seeking to convince. Sometimes years of patient waiting are necessary for our witness to bear fruit.

I like to cook meals for hungry, appreciative people and never have any trouble finding those who like to eat. Gathering around the table with family and friends is always a happy occasion, with everyone in an exuberant mood. I suppose this atmosphere of celebration surrounding such an event is what Jesus had in mind when He told the parable of the "great supper" (Luke 14:16-24).

The happiness of heaven will be like such a feast. I think Jesus wanted us to see just how foolish mankind is. Provision was made for a joyful celebration, but nobody wanted to come. The invitation, sent by the servant was, "Come, for all things are now ready" (v. 17). Our role today is that of servants, announcing Christ's invitation: "Now is the accepted time; behold, now is the day of salvation" (2 Cor. 6:2, KJV).

In the parable, the invitation was received rather coldly. Not a downright refusal, but "they all with one accord began to make excuses" (Luke 14:18). Sound familiar?

The first person wanted to see some land he had bought. The next had bought a team of oxen and had to try them out. These were not bad things to do. Choosing to be busy with our own concerns when we ought to be attending to spiritual matters can easily become a habit.

The last invited guest had a super excuse, probably the most used today. He blamed someone else: "I have married a wife and therefore I cannot come" (Luke 14:20). If we do not want to do something, any excuse will do. Jesus went right to the heart of the matter when he said, "He who is not with Me is against Me, and he who does not gather with Me scatters abroad" (Matt. 12:30).

From the standpoint of our responsibility as the servants who invite, we know that success will always come by God's initiation. Even the best qualified and most faithful can accomplish nothing without the Spirit. "Neither he who plants is anything, nor he who waters, but God who gives the increase" (1 Cor. 3:7). "But God. . . ." Without that possibility, we could not pray for others to be saved, for we ourselves would be lost. Without all of God's exciting possibilities, we could not pray for healing, and many of us can remember times when but for His intervention, we would not be here. And what about the times we were in utter darkness and despair—but God opened a door somewhere to the light, and we could go on.

The following poem was written by Evan Gammial, my brother and a scholar of creative thought.

Lament of the Ancient

The lamp of life is down to dry,
Its flame now flickers low.
The questions, they have all been asked;
The answers we all know.

The clock once wound that ticked so long,
Alas, is now run down.
The field once bright in shining green
Is now in somber brown.

The blood once warm as summer earth
Now courses chill and slow.
The sky-blue sparkle in the eyes
Now barely shows a glow.

The soaring thoughts and secret dreams,
Now dead and dry as dust.
The mighty sword of faith and hope,
Discarded, gathering rust.

Is this then, the fate of man
Whose work has changed the earth
And visited in outer space
In search of other worth?

Yes, this must be the plan for man,
For ever as we fall,
Another lot arrives on time
Unmindful of it all.

Evan said I could I offer these lines in conclusion.

But God designed the flickering lamp;
He wrote the Master Plan—
And He who measured time and space
Also made the man.

Life for all, without the truth
Indeed is cold and grim. . . .
But God, with cords of love, returns
Man's errant heart to Him.

13
Children of Love

But Jesus called them to Him and said, "Let the little children come to Me, and do not forbid them; for of such is the kingdom of God" (Luke 18:16).

I can think of no place in society where people are not deeply concerned about rights and the protection of those rights. Few citizens can quote the first ten amendments to the Constitution known as the Bill of Rights, sweeping prohibitions against government infringement on fundamental rights. Recent years have brought changes in our laws to effect a better system of protecting the rights of ethnic minorities, women, and children. Unfortunately, there is no way to improve the environmental hazards imposed upon many children in their impressionable years.

Jesus spoke of Himself as "the bread of life," "living water," "the light of the world." He also stated that "whoever does not receive the kingdom of God as a little child will by no means enter it" (Luke 18:17). We somehow relate belief to adult comprehension. But some adults can be very "religious" without knowing God. Jesus' experience with the Pharisees made Him quite aware of that.

Jesus probably had some childlike characteristics in mind as prerequisites to receiving the kingdom. Children are usually very inquisitive and very trusting. Many adults, even those who choose to believe, are often not inquisitive enough to search out for themselves the truths of God. No one can fully trust, vicariously. Children learn by example, and our minds must be as receptive to the Spirit as theirs is to the parent's example.

My first baby was a longed-for little boy. In my first moments alone with him, I gave him to the Lord as sincerely as I knew how, believing in my nineteen-year-old simplicity that settled the matter. My faith remains undaunted. I expect a fulfilling life for him.

What our children choose for their life work is not nearly as important as who they choose to focus their lives on. Today our young people are not being encouraged to enter service-oriented occupations. The making of money is being impressed upon our young as a primary goal. Not enough money to live on causes some of today's social problems, but more than enough often increases trouble.

A Father's Thoughts

My son brought at evening, his broken heart to me,
I bowed my head to hide my eyes; I could not let him see
The doubt that I could help, or see my own despair,
We cannot live another's life, however much we care.
If I could rectify mistakes, or see his problems through,
How gladly I would do it and let him start anew;
But this I know, our troubles form a pattern we repeat—
Escaping one, another comes on uninvited feet!
So many of Life's problems magnify and grow
Because we fail to follow the wisdom that we know.
In my son's wrong decisions, the blame is shared by me—
The rebel guiding him today seemed not so bad at three.
I gave him all I had to give of means, and love and learning,

What he needs most I cannot give: the talent of discerning
What is best for him. This, only God can give;
Each man must find it for himself, this knowing how to live.

Speaking softly from our hearts to those we know and love,
Seeing that each circumstance comes to us from above;
Almost all our problems are caused by attitude—
Our day's end is determined by our choice of morning
    mood.

Refreshment for my son must come from One who's never
    weary,
His need is for a lasting hope; my help is temporary . . .
I pray that he will look beyond my feeble, floundering way,
To ask his OTHER FATHER'S strength to guide him
    through the day!

I wrote that poem for a newspaper article and was surprised
when I received several calls about it on the day the paper went
out. The callers all said basically the same thing, "I wish I could
have read that years ago." Our children need to be taught by
example what we consider important.

Some people give children more responsibility than they can
handle. For example, parents may try to make up for what they
missed while growing up by giving their children every material thing possible. Other people give children no responsibility,
blaming parents for whatever trouble young people get themselves into. Neither attitude is very healthy for children.

One of the first lessons a child should learn is to accept personal responsibility for actions. The world is full of people who
have the false idea that others are responsible for how they feel.
This totally evasive concept is the great obstacle to Christian
development. When taught to our children by example, it re-
stricts their developing mature attitudes.

In close relationships, especially with children, the danger is in rewarding wrong actions. When a child is taught—and believe me, he saw it working for somebody—that others are responsible for his happiness, he begins to expect them to always behave the way he wants. When they do not, he feels neglected and unloved. So, he becomes more demanding, more manipulative. Almost all children go through some stages of this without any role model simply because young children are self-centered. That is where parents and other persons important to the children come in.

When Jesus was asked what was necessary to inherit eternal life, this answer was given: "You shall love the Lord your God with all your heart, with all your soul, with all your strength, and with all your mind, and your neighbor as yourself" (Luke 10:27). To "love your neighbor as yourself" involves managing our own feelings and reactions to others. Do we really enjoy the feeling of being a victim of others? That is exactly what we are if they are to blame for our bad feelings.

Parents are accountable for what their children learn from them. If we want our children to have "clean hands and a pure heart," we will teach them to consider these important.

My son Fred was only three when he inadvertently told me something about myself that I have never forgotten. We were ready to go out and I had dressed him first, which was always a mistake. Calling him in from the yard, I was dismayed at all the dirt he had managed to get on himself in five minutes. In exasperation, I asked, "What am I going to do with you? We haven't time for another bath!" In great concern and all earnestness, he said, "Mom, can't you just dust me off?" I have found that this is what most of us want. Instead of real cleansing of soul, we want just a little dusting off.

Our children, so much with us present or absent, are beautifully described in Psalm 127:3-5:

> Behold, children are a heritage from the Lord,
> The fruit of the womb is His reward.
> Like arrows in the hand of a warrior,
> So are the children of one's youth.
> Happy is the man who has his quiver full of them.

Like arrows flying from the bow, their mark will be more sure if the bow is bent by strength from a disciplined arm. Every target reached touches joy to our hearts as nothing else can, and their failures are more grievous to us than our own.

When our children go out into the world for the first time, it may be a great adventure to them. But for those who have nurtured them from infants, it is a chapter ended. Truly the bow that bids the arrow fly, my heart is set on each new goal they dream. I am certain there is nothing unique in my happiness in each small triumph or my pain in each shared sorrow.

When my youngest son went across several states to a school in Florida, we knew he could not come home often. Several months passed before I saw him. Our few days together were, in some vague way, unsatisfying, for he had changed. It was not so much a visible change as a change of mood. I sensed in him a restlessness, a questioning for which I had no answers.

On a dismal, wintry day, I drove him to the airport to return to his studies. Our small talk was punctuated by quick, forced smiles.

Even as I returned home, the words I had not been able to find began to take the shape of a poem in my mind. Walking into the house, I sat down at my desk and poured out my feelings.

Only You Can Find the Handle

I stood and watched as you passed by,
One moment you were there . . .
Then with flashing silver wings

You were gone.
The clouds were thick and gray
As they sullenly denied your presence;
And I was alone.

I shivered as the cold rain fell,
My throat ached with unspoken words,
And as I slowly walked away
My heart was torn . . .
I had not given you Life's greatest need.
The freezing rain ran down my face
And it was warm.

I fully know your doubts, your fears,
For they are mine today
If I can not impart to you
In some scale,
The sure knowledge that they
Who would see the wonders of the deep
Must trust the sail.

Forget the cynic's way of life;
He does not speak your tongue,
The tools God gave for you to use,
Though seeming small,
Entrust to Him; give what you have
And you will find it is enough
To conquer all!

I signed my name and sent the message on its way. Three days later, I answered my telephone to hear my son's voice on the other end, "Your letter came today."

God gave us the capacity to exercise an interchange of impulses between ourselves and others. This reaching out is often wordless. It is not there to master problems, but just to touch.

Actually, its purpose is to put us in touch with the One who always understands us.

John spoke of friends, a clambake on the beach, and a painting he was working on, but I was listening to the confidence in his voice, the assurance that all was well. Just before we hung up, he casually said, "I was curious about one part of the poem. That about the 'wonders of the deep;' is that a quote from somewhere?" You can believe that I was quick to point out where he could read it for himself: "They that go down to the sea in ships, that do business in great waters; These see the works of the Lord, and his wonders in the deep" (Ps. 107:23-24, KJV).

Collectively, Al and I have seven children; not, Al has three, I, four, which happens to be the biological dispensation, but we have seven. This is the children's understanding, too, so naturally the sibling relations between all of them are close and easy. I must refer here to Al's children as such, but only for the purpose of identification.

We recognize that we are all very different. This difference is in life-style as well as personality, but instead of division, it creates interest in each other. From the beginning, I wanted it to be that way. I knew full well that I could not create unity, no matter how worthy a goal. But it was well within God's reach. "For with God nothing will be impossible" (Luke 1:37).

When Al announced without preamble that he was getting married, it must have shocked his family, for he had sworn repeatedly that he would never remarry. Not one of them knew me. (I think the announcement was made at the dinner table, which was almost overturned in the excitement.) Right away, the elder son dispatched himself to "check me out."

Kenneth and I were great friends from the start. His dropping by for a quick cup of coffee because he happened to be in the neighborhood has always amused his dad and me, for he had to drive 140 miles to get in the neighborhood. The quick cup of coffee turned into one of the most treasured afternoons of my life. What sweeter memory is there than when we find, in friendship, a rare, kindred soul!

The abiding love that exists among the rest of us was a gradual unfolding with the others. Who can say why? This is the individual difference I spoke of. Various personalities are developed from backgrounds usually unknown to us, but they are always occasion for exploration.

I immediately saw the need to have the same honest, open relationship with these children who were not my own by birth that I had with those who were. That is a lot easier said than done, for we seek to protect ourselves from others. To open ourselves to others is not only painful but also painstaking. To really know others, to know what makes them sad or why they are inconsistent in their reactions to certain things or to understand their points of sensitivity; all these are impossible to absorb quickly. Because it takes time for people to know each other will, we try to protect ourselves from real and imaginary harm.

The bitterness that sometimes exists among members of the same family may not be supported by all, but all will suffer an association loss. Sisters and brothers who allow their pride to alienate them from each other rob themselves of joys they can never recapture. Pride is a hard taskmaster who pays off in counterfeit coin. "By pride comes only contention" is never more clearly fulfilled than among stiff-necked family members. Many of the bitter feelings within families could be removed if someone would take the responsibility of working for unity. One person can make the difference if Christ is working His wisdom and His power through that one who has offered himself.

Within our immediate family structure, some difficulty was avoided by our family's singular goal: Al's happiness (of first concern to his children) and my happiness (of first concern to mine). A pleasant meeting ground is always easier found when everyone has a mind to converge on a central goal. Under other arrangements of our own initiation, we would all have tried to love each other for the sake of the committment Al and I had made. God had a better arrangement. Under it, each is loved by all the others for his or her individual sake.

In times of need, the immature Christian is likely to attempt to fit God's Word to the situation. Sometimes with great difficulty, and always with great soul-searching, we come to the place of fitting our situation to God's Word. It requires more discipline of self than we think we can bear, but that first step is the hardest.

When God sees the purpose, our desire to follow Him, He takes the burden off our backs. This is the yoke Jesus offered: "Take My yoke upon you and learn from Me, for I am gentle and lowly in heart, and you will find rest for your souls. For My yoke is easy and My burden is light" (Matt. 11:29-30). Have you thought of gentleness and humility as weaknesses? Of all human attributes, these stand proven as the strongest!

In the process of getting to know others who will be a day-to-day part of our lives, we often give too much attention to what we extract from others. We look at each little reaction to what we say and do as if it were a final judgment. Relationships will improve if our concentration is on what we are allowing others to get from us. As we, through love, come to better understanding of each other, it is surprising how much the interchange of rhetoric is altered. Our Bill keeps us all laughing with his sometimes caustic wit. But before we found this easy camaraderie, he would have guarded against so freely voicing his more personal banter.

I consider a genuine closeness with children to be the cornerstone of character building. We see evidence that the violated rights of young children become the pivot of their violating the rights of others in later years. There seems not to be an infallible system of training children to grow into fine Christian men and women. A look at the parable of the prodigal son shows us the variance in two sons who grew up under the same roof.

So what we do is set up a minisystem of what God set for humanity when He gave Moses the law. We care for children with tenderness and affection and insist that they obey certain rules. Teaching obedience with patience is never simple, but well worth everything we invest in it. Only those adults who learned to accept discipline in childhood will be able to discipline themselves.

The very young do not protect themselves from others as adults do. The need for protection develops from feeling hurt. That protectiveness can only be removed by love that is constant.

When we give our best but somehow fail to accomplish the good we set out to do, the story of the prodigal encourages us to not give up. The story tells us what the son was doing while he was away, wasting his life in riotous living. Nothing is said of what the father was doing all that time, but we are given a graphic picture of his attitude at the time of the son's return. In the father's words to the returning prodigal and to the elder son, the loving response of a gracious Heavenly Father is seen. No one knows but God how many prayers were offered up by that earthly father before his son returned from "the far country."

Romans 13:8 is a positive and somewhat cryptic message: "Owe no one anything except to love one another, for he who loves another has fulfilled the law." We are all familiar with the discomfort of being in debt for material things that money can buy. We seldom consider the greater debts we owe. We are only stewards of whatever talent, wisdom, or grace we have. To those in authority, we owe respect; to our parents, honor. This kind of indebtedness is never fully paid. But pleasure can be found in the delivery of each installment. Every little act of kindness we show returns to us the greater blessing. To love is a debt everyone owes. It is a debt that no one will ever fully pay.

Families today are often a mix from several divorces. Children frequently have to deal with emotional problems they might not have had if parents had not divorced. To further complicate matters, occurrences within a family can trigger feelings from past experiences. Have there not been times when the sudden whistle of a train or the scent of wood smoke or an almost forgotten melody rings a bell in your mind and you were momentarily transported back in time and mood? Grownups have trouble sorting out these disturbing elements. For children, it is often painfully difficult to reconcile the present to their past.

My dad used to tell about a time when his horse broke out of the pasture and wandered away. He inquired of the neighbors, and searched the surrounding pastures, but no one had seen the horse. An older man living just down the road came leading the horse home one morning. Of course, my dad wanted to know where the man had found "old Jude." "Well," the old man chuckled, "I just sort of figured out where I'd go for grazin' if I wuz old Jude and it wuz this dry. I went down to the swamp by the river, and there he wuz." He found Jude by using "horse sense." When our "children of love" are in trouble, it becomes necessary to figure out what they are feeling before we can give the kind of help they need.

14
Know the Word

All Scripture is given by inspiration of God, and is profitable for doctrine, for reproof, for correction, for instruction in righteousness, that the man of God may be complete, thoroughly equipped for every good work (2 Tim. 3:16-17).

So much is said in the Bible on the subject of knowing God's Word that this chapter could stand on Scripture alone. Just the Bible's promises should be enough to motivate us to spend our lives studying it. But somehow, very few believers give serious Bible study high priority. We do this not because God is unimportant to us but because we have convinced ourselves that crying before Him and talking about Him amounts to the same thing as knowing Him. If this were true, Jesus would not have emphasized Matthew 7:21: "Not everyone who says to Me, 'Lord, Lord,' shall enter the kingdom of heaven, but he who does the will of My Father in heaven."

We all sometimes give our time and energies to unprofitable pursuits, for very few ventures have built-in guarantees of success. There is that guarantee in Bible study. If we want principles by which to live, it is in the Bible. If we get off course, our stopgap is there and the reassurances so necessary to peace of soul. God wants our success first of all, "that the man of God may be complete." Only when we are "thoroughly equipped" are we able to do the work that we are here for.

In studying the Bible, we must remember that it is all related to itself. We cannot pull out verses at random and try to fit them into what we want them to say. I have used selected verses throughout this book to illustrate certain points, but these portions were never used out of the context of their original meaning. They were used only to illuminate the same truth they spoke in the Scriptures.

The entire Holy Canon is linked together. It is a progressive unfolding of truth. The Bible is consistent within itself. It reveals God from century through century. Its prophecies are fulfilled. The unrefutable veracity with which one writer after another, under inspiration of God, recorded a perfect union of doctrine is the proof of truth to every child of God. The declaration of Ecclesiastes 8:5 that "a wise man's heart discerns both time and judgment" agrees with Paul's announcement that "with the heart one believes to righteousness, and with the mouth confession is made to salvation" (Rom. 10:10). One who is wise knows that when the clarion call of judgment comes we can send no one in our stead; no bribe we can offer for a reprieve.

All Christians seem to talk a lot to God. If He is not saying anything to us, it must be because we are not listening. We know that "God is Spirit, and those who worship Him must worship in spirit and truth" (John 4:23). We cannot expect to hear Him consistently unless we study His Word. We must steep our minds in it! One day when we are ready, He will begin to communicate with us, moment by moment.

God reveals Himself through His Word. He can do it any way He chooses, but I do not believe that just because I am too lazy or too indifferent to search out His wisdom He is going to apply a great supernatural revelation to my case. In a time of my need

He may—but I cannot count on that until I have used the means He has already given—the Word!

An occasional "pick the magic number" method does not work. The Bible cannot be opened at random in the hope of being directed to "our word from God" for a particular problem. Just because the Book falls open at the place where Peter was instructed to take money from a fish's mouth to pay the Temple tax, I cannot expect to pay my taxes this way. If we are not looking for a particular Scripture, we can sometimes get refreshing little surprises by this method of reading; but the method in itself is no panacea. Occasional reading will never accomplish our desired goal of understanding God's personal message to us.

According to the dictionary, intellect is that power of the mind that thinks and learns. The mind itself is an aggregate of brain processes that includes the ability to feel and will and reason. We think of those who engage sound logic as unusually intelligent individuals of keen mentality. Is it not true that the normal powers of perception can be more sharply honed by practice and that the most ordinary mind can be transformed to loftier concepts?

Not one of us has the right to remain at our present level. The very fact of our being here implies purpose, and logic tells us that the purpose has to be more than to attain perishable things. Those we call great are often people of humble backgrounds who have rightly responded to their calling. Romans 12:2 has everyone's name on it: "Do not be conformed to this world, but be transformed by the renewing of your mind, that you may prove what is that good and acceptable and perfect will of God."

This transformation is a change of the quality of our thinking and not the substance of it. We receive new dispositions and new motivations which give us new hearts and new spirits. We put off "the old man with his deeds," and put on "the new man who is renewed in knowledge according to the image of Him who created him" (Col. 3:9-10). We have no power to work this change, so our part is to open our minds to the Holy Spirit's influence. God creates the "new man" but we must put it on.

The result is that we prove to ourselves and others that God's will for us is perfect because it cannot be improved upon. It is good in the sight of others; and it is always good for us. The final effect is in the peace of knowing that we please God, that He accepts us.

If we are to develop the powers of the mind to its highest level of performance, we must learn to deal with all our working parts: body, mind, and spirit. How can we expect to do that if we neglect the growth of even one part?

I know that in the beginning we may have to force ourselves to search the Scriptures, but along the way something happens. An unexplainable, dynamic power goes to work within us, beginning to open up the dark caverns of our minds that have been closed because we have denied their existence. In the deep of God's thoughts, we find exciting treasures to make us rich. This is better than a promise; it is an already established fact, there for the claiming. I worked out a simple little table to remind me of what Bible study is and what it does.

S—Search the Scriptures (see John 5:39).

T—Treasure hidden (see Matt. 13:44).

U—Unsearchable riches of Christ (see Eph. 3:8).

D—Daily loading us with benefits (see Ps. 68:19).

Y—Yields peaceable fruit of righteousness (see Heb. 12:11).

Employing memory devices helps us to store up Scriptures for future reference. Familiarizing ourselves with the Bible is not to accumulate more doctrine or to acquire a better standard of judgment, though these things are certain to happen. It is to bring our spirits into line with the Lord's, so He can reveal Himself to us and through us. Once we have absorbed a specific portion of God's Word, we suddenly find that it is no longer just knowledge but a power constantly at work conforming us to His image.

To better understand the importance of reverent Bible study, we need to know exactly what we are dealing with. "For the word of God is living and powerful, and sharper than any two-edged sword, piercing even to the division of soul and spirit, and of joints and marrow, and is a discerner of the thoughts and intents of the heart" (Heb. 4:12).

A young boy whose last name the world may never know, was born without immunity to disease. In the hope that treated bone marrow would provide his body with the necessary immunity, a transplant procedure was carried out. After the transplant, the boy's system was unable to resist the attack of the transplant lymphocytes (white blood cells) on his blood-forming tissue. Although the implant was not successful for him, in many rare diseases, healing has resulted for others.

We think of bone disease as being most difficult to treat because of composition of bone is so complex. In the bone marrow tissue, all our red blood cells and blood platelets originate.

As impenetrable as the marrow and bone seem, this "sword of the Word" that cuts both ways has sharpness capable of separating one from the other. Such preciseness cuts through the outer rigid structure to the life-sustaining force within the central core, dividing the two component elements. The analogy this Scripture draws between the basic properties of our being requires careful study to even begin to see its outer edges of truth. I find the relation of marrow to joints no more complex than that of spirit to soul. Our own cleverness will never find out the truth of God; only in humility before Him will we learn who He is. And it is His Word, this two-edged sword, that cuts through our foolish thoughts to the true intents of our hearts. This Word is alive and powerful enough to enter where nothing else can, dividing wisdom from our lack of understanding and obedience from our rebellion. This delicate surgery on the sick psyche, where the good and the bad are mixed together, is for our restoring to health. And hallelujah, our physician has never lost a patient!

If our bone marrow stopped reproducing the vitalizing red blood cells, our bodies would soon become diseased and die. For the Spirit to cease its work would be just as fatal to the soul.

We are born again through faith in Christ which is revealed in God's Word. "So then faith comes by hearing, and hearing by the word of God" (Rom. 10:17). The starting point of our faith is the Bible. It is the point from which our growth progresses, but it is also the point to which we keep returning in a never-ending circle that reaches farther and farther out, "being confident of this very thing, that He who has begun a good work in you will complete it until the day of Jesus Christ" (Phil. 1:6).

If we want more faith, we need to remember the basic tenet that nothing scripturally promised is ever reversed. The Bible states that we get faith by "hearing," and this hearing is not just a perceiving of sound but an acceding responsiveness. And not hearing "every wind of doctrine, by the trickery of men" (Eph. 4:14) but letting "the word of Christ dwell in you richly in all wisdom, teaching and admonishing one another in psalms and hymns and spiritual songs, singing with grace in your hearts to the Lord" (Col. 3:16). I like the thought of the Word of Christ dwelling in us "richly." His Word at times has lived in some of us poorly, with little power, influencing no one. It is more than a matter of just "keeping house" here; we must keep it well with wisdom and grace.

Without the steadying influence of a clear knowledge of what God's Word is, we fall easily into an easy glum, easy glow pattern of looking at circumstances as the final word. Without the knowledge of the power His Word has to change us, we are tempted to give up on ourselves. Knowing the Word is the motivation of our outward perspective. "Therefore we do not lose heart. Even though our outward man is perishing, yet the inward man is being renewed day by day" (2 Cor. 4:16).

Our Two Natures

Two men, Lord, to walk before men
For all the world to see—
One walks by sight; the other by faith,
That he, an example might be.

In the eyes of one there's a flash of wrath
When things disappoint and go wrong;
The eyes of the other are wise and calm—
He trusts You, Lord, and is strong!

One's voice can cut to the heart like a knife,
Carelessly, sorrow it sows—
The other with words, strives to bless and lift,
Sowing kindness wherever he goes

False pride in one sets him up as a judge
To see fault in the lives of others—
The man of faith looks out with love
Seeing all men as his brothers.

Have you seen these two, so unlike in ways?
Have you wondered how it can be
That they dwell together under one cloak?
Forgive me, Lord . . . they are me!

Help me to subdue that sight-walking man
Who puts You to shame with his sin.
Give me the power to conquer myself
That I may be a blessing to men!

"The grass withers, the flower fades,
  But the word of our God stands forever"

(Isa. 40:8).

15
The Gifts and the Giver

For who makes you differ from another? And what do you have
that you did not receive? Now if you did indeed receive it, why
do you glory as if you had not received it? (1 Cor. 4:7).

Jesus said, "I am the vine, you are the branches. He who
abides in me, and I in him, bears much fruit; for without me you
can do nothing" (John 15:5). In those times when I have nursed
within myself a mean, selfish, unforgiving spirit, those words
have burned into me like live coals. At no time is their truth
more convincing than when my sin has shut me out from the
Lord's presence. I think we have to experience the pain of the
separation to fully realize the joy of the union.

When we are given new life, it is complete salvation. But a
new Christian is like a baby—birth is the beginning of the journey to maturity. Have we learned how to know if we are abiding in Christ? We can see it as a swinging door that opens both
ways: faith opening it inward to receive Christ and love swinging it outward toward man. Through our faith He abides in us;
through our love we abide in Him. The door has to open constantly both ways or the balance between His abiding and our
abiding will be broken. "Faith without works is dead" (Jas. 2:20);
so if the door is only open to faith, the ministry love gives is lost.
"Though I bestow all my goods to feed the poor, and though I

give my body to be burned, but have not love, it profits me nothing" (1 Cor. 13:3). Faith and love must balance each other; they must both be operative. Love is the "works" Jesus gave us to do. It is clearly this abiding that Paul was speaking of when he said, "It is no longer I who live, but Christ lives in me" (Gal. 2:20).

Let us face it—some people are just not easy to love. This is not meant in a defamatory way. There are many otherwise lovely, generous people who have not submitted their self-love to Christ's control, so they remain overly sensitive and intolerant. I know of but one way to handle them—just grit your teeth and concentrate on Jesus Christ and His gift to you. Even when all we show to the difficult ones is love, we have no guarantee that it will change them to having a less abrasive attitude. But when I take this action, it does change me—and it is the kind of change that is a definite improvement. If we are spitefully attacked by another, we have only two options. We can respond in like manner, or we can refuse to be drawn into the vineyard of sour grapes cultivated by others.

A young man once told me of an experience that often reminds of this. We all have known those who were very adept at cutting remarks. This young man was being unfairly maligned by such a person. He felt himself becoming more frustrated and angry by the moment. Right in the midst of the tirade, instead of striking back, he did some quick, inward reasoning. He said to himself, *Here I was in a wonderful mood until someone chose to apply the pressure of his own rotten temperament. Now why should anyone else make me less than I am? My reasons for feeling good still exist. My attitude can only be changed if I allow it!* It worked for him, and it will work for us. Others can speak unkindly, but they can not decide our response. We are responsible for that.

We are perpetual recipients of God's generosity, much of

which can be seen at a glance. Some gifts are less obvious, but their resulting blessing is apparent to all. We call these spiritual gifts, and concerning them, Paul said, "Brethren, I do not want you to be ignorant" (1 Cor. 12:1). He explained that, prior to the grace of God in their lives, the Corinthians were following the herd and being carried away by the grossest idolatry. In any situation, it is wise of us to remember where we came from. When we are cognizant of our former condition, it becomes much easier to recognize what we have been given.

The various kinds of gifts all come from the same Spirit; and if we are in Christ, we all have received at least one spiritual gift. As Christ is one body, we are all members of that body with one principle of life. The least significant of us can ill afford to say, "My gift is not as great as that of others, so I won't use it. What good is it when others can do so much more?" Now, I really think my eyes are of more benefit to me than my ears; but if I stuff my ears full of cotton because they seem less useful to me than my eyes, I will miss a great contribution to my overall perspective. So the least gifted of believers is important in the family of God.

I used to actually hunger for a thrilling voice with which to sing praises. A friend who sings once told me that I probably get a lot more enjoyment from music because of my inability to produce it. Variety in a body is the quality that makes it interesting, and our diversity of gifts enhances the beauty of the whole. That voice I longed for would have been considered by me to be a marvelous gift. Actually, it is a talent, a particular aptitude for a specific activity. All talent in a sense is a gift, and all spiritual gifts endow the recipient with aptitude for enlightening and improving. "Even so you, since you are zealous for spiritual gifts, let it be for the edification of the church that you seek to excel" (1 Cor. 14:12). All our talents are to be used to strengthen the church.

How many of us know for certain the particular gift entrusted to us for the betterment of others? In Romans and in 1 Corinthians, spiritual gifts are listed and explained. Is there a way for us to know which of these we have? Of course there is. "The manifestation of the Spirit is given to each one for the profit of all" (1 Cor. 12:7). There would be no reason to give us this manifestation if there were no way for us to use it.

Before we can find out what our call to service is, we must resolve something. We must decisively act to give our minds and bodies over to God's direction. "I beseech you therefore, brethren, by the mercies of God, that you present your bodies a living sacrifice, holy, acceptable to God, which is your reasonable service" (Rom. 12:1). Is it reasonable to expect us to be holy? That is what His Word says; it is just sane and logical for us to be holy. In fact, it is the normal state of the Christian because as He who called you is holy, you also be holy in all your conduct, because it is written, 'Be holy for I am holy' " (1 Pet. 1:15-16).

Christians today are either embarrassed by the thought that they could be holy or they dismiss it as a human impossibility. Either way, we are in trouble. We are not very clear on what holiness is. The dictionary defines holiness as "having spiritual worth." We know that God's holiness is perfect. Paul spoke of the Spirit of God living in us, perfecting us. "Therefore, having these promises, beloved, let us cleanse ourselves from all filthiness of the flesh and spirit, perfecting holiness in the fear of God" (2 Cor. 7:1).

Isn't holiness, then, the inner fire that lights us outwardly in a manifestation of grace? According to Paul, we do the house cleaning, banishing the filth from our minds and hearts so that we can be filled with God's saving grace. Our "balm in Gilead" works its healing first in us, then reaches out to others through us.

Speaking to believers, John said that although we do not now know exactly what we shall be we do know "that when He is revealed, we shall be like Him, for we shall see Him as He is." He then gave this qualification: "Everyone who has this hope in Him purifies himself, just as He is pure." (1 John 3:2-3).

Our spiritual faith not just sitting there inside us but set on fire to burn out the secret sin and proud ego is holiness.

As parents we correct our children, even as we were corrected by our parents. The submission to this becomes less disagreeable as respect for the authority figure is learned. "Shall we not much more readily be in subjection to the Father of spirits and live?" (Heb. 12:9). Our Father's chastening is "for our profit, that we may be partakers of His holiness" (v. 10). We are further instructed to "pursue peace with all men, and holiness, without which no one will see the Lord" (v. 14). Many whose hope is in Christ have too long excused themselves with the mistaken idea that the Lord, knowing all about their human weakness, does not expect very much of them. He does understand our natural lack of moral strength, but what He expects from us is not dependant on that. His directive will for us is always based on His ability, not ours. In our need, we can echo Psalm 138:3:

> In the day when I cried out,
>   You answered me,
> And made me bold with strength in my
>   in my soul.

How many times have we fallen back on that tremendous promise of Isaiah 41:10?

> Fear not, for I am with you;
> Be not dismayed, for I am your God.
> I will strengthen you,
> Yes, I will help you,

I will uphold you with My righteous
right hand.

Some may well say, "Yes, I know all that; I have submitted
and I am committed—but I am still not sure what spiritual gift
the Lord has given me to use." To anyone in this dilemma of
uncertainty, I can only offer my own experience as a testimony.
When I was very young, I often felt an emptiness within me that
nothing seemed to satisfy. Because of my lack of instruction
about a Heavenly Father, I recognized my sense of need as no
more than a hunger for something, undefined and unexplainable. One day as I struggled against this inner emotion, the Lord
quietly moved into my emptiness and filled me with the assurance that I need never know that hunger again.

As I grew up, three desires grew in my heart, two of which
I questioned for years. The first, to walk with God, is obviously
the first desire of every Christian. The other two, to be a teacher
and to be a writer, almost disappeared from sight in my pursuit
of what seemed all that was accessible to me. I married right
out of high school, gave birth to four children over a period of
years, and became a very busy, happy wife and mother. If I
forgot my second and third ambitions, the Lord did not. You
see, those desires of our hearts do not just happen; God plants
them there! He cannot fail; when He plants a desire in our
hearts, He has all the resources needed to accomplish it.

A friend, who was also my Sunday School teacher, went out
of town for a weekend and asked me to teach her class. I did
it, but no one can know how tongue-tied and inept I felt. I hope
my sincerity overshadowed my incompetence. Being kind, the
members were uncomplaining, as we can all afford to be as long
as someone else is willing to do the job. I have found that if we
really want to serve God, He will see that we have opportunity
and training. Once I agreed to substitute as a teacher, I was

amazed how often I was asked to fill a place. It never occurred to me that the Lord planned it that way.

My older children and their friends were instrumental in drawing me into attempting to express my thoughts in writing. I had become the leader of their Bible study department, and one of my duties was to present a time of devotion each Sunday. Because I knew their needs and interests, the impersonal materials provided sometimes did not fit, so I began writing in little adaptations. Again, it never occurred to me that everything was proceeding according to the Lord's plan, for in all this, I never thought of myself as being either a teacher or a writer.

My purpose in telling this experience is not to convince the reader that I either write or teach well, though I try to do my best in both areas. My point is, a writer writes; a teacher teaches —and that is what I do. These are the spiritual gifts my Heavenly Father gave me to use, and I found out about them by simply yielding myself to His leading. I believe that He meant it to be just that simple: first planting the desire, then opening the door. You know what you are best at doing; you know what just seems to come naturally to you. There are many talents I might like if left to myself, but the Lord helps us in making our choices.

All spiritual gifts are intended to lift up Christ to others. Though we are to desire spiritual gifts, we are given "a more excellent way" of serving. "Though I speak with the tongues of men and of angels, but have not love, I have become as sounding brass or a clanging cymbal. And though I have the gift of prophecy, and understand all mysteries and all knowledge, and though I have all faith, so that I could remove mountains, but have not love, I am nothing" (1 Cor. 13:1-2). To love, indeed, is the universal gift; this love in practice typifies Christian excellence.

God asks, "Whom shall I send, And who will go for Us?" (Isa. 6:8). If we love, there is only one answer we can give:

The Silent Lost

One day I stood alone,
A precipice broke sheer beneath my feet;
I saw no end, so black it was—
My stretched forth hand no other hand could meet.

I saw forms of people
Moving single file along the edge,
Blindly treading air they fell
As I stood frozen to the grassy ledge.

I wondered why no man
Called out to turn them from their doom;
Grasping emptiness, they went without a sound—
And I still waited, in the shadowed gloom.

Then a stumbling child
Clutched at a tuft of grass, and I could see
The roots give way, and as they went,
Her pleading eyes and hands reached out to me!

My ears, at last were opened;
The voice of God, like thunder, broke free—
"Whom shall I send, and who will go for Us?"
With broken heart I cried, "Send me; send me!"

Christians in our age love their church buildings. Who can deny it when we see the majestic structures with their elaborate appointments? I agree with beauty in our places of worship, but I wonder if maybe some believe that God just waits there in the building for people to come and find Him. We must take care not to love our church buildings and organizations more than we love people.

I have a friend of whom it was said, "I have never been with her that she did not give me something good to take away with me." I, also, can say this of my friend, Amy, for she uses the gift of words to bless lives. An encouraging word here, a comforting one there, but always the fitly spoken word "like apples of gold in pictures of silver" (Prov. 25:11, KJV). What a remarkable gift! It is within the reach of every person to give something of the spirit; to fulfill in some measure the purpose of God's giving to us. Develop the gift! Guard the tongue! Failing to use our gifts, we stand to lose them, and in that loss is the danger of becoming useless. Paul said, "Therefore I run thus: not with uncertainty. Thus I fight: not as one who beats the air. But I discipline my body, and bring it under subjection, lest, when I have preached to others, I myself should become disqualified" (1 Cor. 9:26-27). To think of the implications of that word, "disqualified," stirs me to immediate action, though it does not mean that we lose our salvation. A disqualified athlete is still a member of the team; he is just no longer useful to it.

16
That's a Wrap

For He shall give His angels charge
  over you,
To keep you in all your ways.
They shall bear you up in their hands,
Lest you dash your foot against a
  stone (Ps. 91:11-12).

In current jargon, "a wrap" means that all points have been made; all bases are covered. That is our situation when our standing with Christ is secure. Surrounded by Christ's love, power, and wisdom, we are wrapped in the grace of all His attributes. Every believer in Jesus Christ should know that he possesses these things. If he does, why in the world doesn't he act like it?

First of all, not all are good actors. And even the great ones will break down in the raw unrehearsed scenes. You see, life was never intended to be a stage; only man's duplicity attempts to make it so. We all at times go into our little acts, pretending concern where there is none, feigning good health when we feel bad, tolerating people and situations we would choose to avoid. Analyzing the motivation behind some of these performances would be interesting. But the point is, we justify such acting because it expresses what we know we ought to feel. We are known by our fruit. "Even so, every good tree bears good fruit, but a bad tree bears bad fruit" (Matt. 7:17). The Christian knows that he will not always feel like doing what is right, but he also knows that his fruit is not dependent upon how he feels, but on what he is. God's compelling force interacts with the Christian's own conscious commitment to produce the fruit. That explains the conclusion of Jesus in verse 18: "A good tree cannot bear bad fruit, nor can a bad tree bear good fruit." If Christ abides in us and we abide in Him, our reaction to a situation is never an act. It is a natural outgrowth of commitment.

We sometimes wail that life is too short for one cut off in the mainstream of living. How can this be said when God knows the end of every person and has the power over life and death? If an ending here seems premature to us, it is because we cannot see what lies ahead. We do not see the blessing God gives because we cannot know the alternative consequence. When death calls, life here should be considered complete. Sadly, for many, it is only final.

My son John, in explaining the process of learning to paint in the art school he attended, showed me several subjects he was working on. I thought they were terrific. He insisted that they still required much work. When I said they looked finished to me, he replied, "The painting is made up of values. After it is well begun, the entire subject is developed, stroke by stroke, but never in a piecemeal fashion. All parts of the whole are effected progressively so that, at any time, I could stop and consider it a finished work." As our Master Artist develops each canvas, He also knows when it is time to stop. He knows when that last brush stroke reaches its zenith of beauty and strength. Beyond that, to add more would only take away.

I knew a man who was horribly crushed by falling rock. For a long time Prentice's survival was in doubt. Eventually he recovered enough to leave the hospital, though he was paralyzed from his neck down. Unable even to feed himself, this man lived for fourteen years in this helpless condition.

In the last years of his life, I visited with him occasionally, sometimes by telephone. The visits meant much to both of us. His spontaneous humor was a delight, and it was always present. Prentice was also capable of deep intellectual thought and often spoke seriously of politics, business dealings, and religion. One day in conversation, he said, "Some people have a warped idea of what they are here for. We are not here just to have a good time or to make a good living or even to do a good job. We are here to become what we ought to be." I agreed but went on to say that if we became what we ought to be those other things usually followed. He answered, "That is not important—it is what God is making of us that counts." Very earnestly, he continued, "I know that I would never have changed, had this not happened to me. I would have gone right on the way I was. Believe me; God does know best." I, of course, had no idea what he was like before the accident. He knew.

In the few years I knew Prentice, I saw him endure suffering beyond belief. I saw him bear up under the shattering tragedy of his only son's death in an accident similar to his own. Through it all, he remained calm and sane. Underneath, like a wellspring of living water, that marvelous spirit sparkled. In his last conscious moments, unable to speak, he managed a smile.

Prentice's family and friends were disappointed that he left this life without regaining the ability to walk again, for that had been his dream for fourteen years. Maybe his soul was more beautiful in that wheelchair; who knows? I am convinced of this: some day we will see Prentice walking!

Do you want the Lord to take you in for His own?

Do you want to know the joy of His presence?

Do you want to help others find the abundant life?

Do you want to go to heaven?

I am certain that anyone who has read this far will answer all four questions in the affirmative, for a negative answer makes no sense at all. There is a fifth, very important question: Is this all you want? Some will ask, perhaps, "What more can there be?" If you accept the words of Jesus as the ultimate authority, there is this: "You shall love the Lord your God with all your heart, with all your soul, and with all your mind" (Matt. 22:37). When this great, encompassing commandment becomes your truth, all your "wants" will consolidate into the mature Christian answer, "Only what Christ wants!"

You Can Open the Door

Clouds may oppress, darkness may come,
Deep shadows may make your path dim;
Don't sit and wait for the day to grow clear,
You can walk by faith with Him!

Great knowledge may not be yours to share,
Your strength may be limited, too—
If you have no special talent to give
There is still a job for you.

Deprived and alone, many grope in the dark
Who need to be told there is more,
Imprisoned in fear, with no key but you—
Be the one who opens the door!

We often keep our experiences of faith hidden. If we can do nothing else, we can tell someone of a crucial time when only God could help us, and He did. First opening the door of faith between ourselves and God, we are then able to open the door for others.

God's Word teaches that He wants to bring us to the place where we can know Him as our God. When we reach the point at which all else would be meaningless without Him, we are ready for Him to begin the exciting revelation of Himself through us. At that stage of Christian development, life becomes almost more than a body can contain. Like sparkling waters in a country creek, our spiritual joy surges through whatever we have to do. "Your Word was to me the joy and rejoicing of my heart; For I am called by your name, O Lord God of hosts" (Jer. 15:16). When the eyes of our spirit within meet God's, we find that even the most mundane duties take on an esthetic wonder. Within ourselves, we become what we believe and truly reflect His image.

Saved, surrendered, serving—that is the ideal order of life. Unfortunately, this order is juggled by many in their attempt to serve before becoming surrendered. It is easy to say we love God, and we can believe it as long as we can look at Him in a rather abstract way that does not require us to deal with Him. But when we trust God enough to draw close, we find that surrender is the only thing that will satisfy the consuming hunger and thirst that we feel.

Some people take longer than others before being able to fully surrender to God. We can gain some understanding of this by reading the Book of Job. I was frightened for years by the fact that terrible things could happen to Job while he loved and obeyed God. My incomplete concept of God required that He reward me visibly for love and service. I finally managed to overcome my fear enough to actually study the book, and right in front of my eyes the picture began to change. True faith recognizes that God can work in all things for our good (see Rom. 8:28). I learned that though God had given Job many blessings, Job would have revered God without them as his endurance through later tribulation proves.

We all love certain people, but we must reach the place in Christian maturity where we love all people for Christ's sake.

We who love Him are His human contact with people. It is easy to praise God when His blessings are visible. Where are our praises when disaster strikes? If we love God, we trust Him as much in the darkness as we do in the light. When we finally learn to trust God's love, surrender becomes easy. Knowing "that all things work together for good to those who love God, to those who are the called according to His purpose," we unreservedly give ourselves over to Him for whatever He chooses.

If we really want to rid ourselves of shallow, shackled lives, we are going to have to stop depending on our quick application of a few verses of Scripture by rote and another organizational meeting to learn new methods of operation. These have never worked. The only method that will work is an immediate, urgent, stirring up the gift within.

Go to the Source for your instructions; they are all there in the spiritual standards of the Word.

> Ho! Everyone who thirsts,
> Come to the waters;
> And you who have no money,
> Come, buy and eat.
> Yes, come buy wine and milk
> Without money and without price. (Isa. 55:1).